FUTURE FORCE

Kids that Want To, Can, and Do!

originally Deve teachers

8J
FOUNDATION PRINCIPALS
7 STEPS → PDSA
System
Customers
Variation

understand missions → purpose

HTTP//.WWW.

time and graph
new data

1st time: 34 piece puzzle in baggie
2nd time: Now you know what it looks like – mix up & put back together
3rd time: Use puzzle cover

Puzzle activity
to see how clean 1,2,3 and easy to have clean aim
discuss tools
Standards – goals
share missions
+dis
make action plan
implement
reflect and analyze data

A TEACHER'S HANDBOOK

ELAINE McCLANAHAN and CAROLYN WICKS

Illustrations by Jeff Owens

10 9 8 7 6 5 4 3 2

ISBN 1-882180-09-7

Griffin Publishing
544 Colorado Street
Glendale, California 91204

Manufactured in the United States of America.

FOREWORD

FOREWORD

This book is a refreshing relief from the torrent of books and articles, in which we are now awash, which tell us how bad things are and admonish us to do better. Carolyn and Elaine have taken a different tack. Their book tells beleaguered teachers what to do, how to do it and what to expect as they do it.

They are not like some researchers I know who rush into print to describe theories they have never put into practice. Instead, the authors exhibit the patience and humor of practitioners who have learned by doing and are keenly aware of the problems faced by beginners.

The introduction of quality principles in the classroom requires teachers and students to regard each other in new ways. The current buzzwords are "to adopt a new paradigm." That's a tough assignment. This book takes you by the hand and, with numerous examples and helpful hints, encourages you to try.

While it is true that the introduction of these methods does require extra time at the beginning of a semester, the time is more than made up for later in the same semester. If these tools are taught to all students in the lower grades, the impact in later years will be enormous. The cumulative effect from K through 12 will change our world. I have no doubt about that.

President Hutchins of the University of Chicago once said, "No one knows what we could do with education, because we have never really tried." So please, read this book and try it. You'll like it.

Dr. Myron Tribus

FROM BUSINESS AND INDUSTRY TO EDUCATION...

Most companies integrating these skills and tools would attribute their motivation to the Total Quality Management (TQM) movement of the 1980s. As U.S. industries began to feel the impact of global competition, many industrial leaders turned to the guidance of Dr. W. Edwards Deming.

Dr. Deming introduced a set of principles that taught business and industries to break down barriers, eliminate fear, and encourage a focus on process. These principles are not only helping the U.S. industrial base to continuously improve, but are also being implemented in the educational system.

Dr. Myron Tribus, an admirer and colleague of Dr. Deming, passionately believes in the benefits to be derived by integrating the principles of TQM in our schools and dedicates much of his effort to achieving this.

Dr. Tribus has written several articles praising the efforts of schools implementing total quality concepts. One school in particular that has captured the attention of Dr. Tribus is a small high school in Sitka, Alaska. Mt. Edgecumbe High School has developed an approach which impacts every level within the school.

- The superintendent envisions creating autonomous team players by helping students develop self-esteem.

- Teachers are learning quality tools and techniques in special workshops.

- Students and staff have developed a mission statement for the school.

- Students help one another to become independent learners.

Acknowledgments

We really enjoyed writing this book. What can we say? We really believe in this stuff. We've worked hard. We've put in tedious hours, we've bickered, we've cussed, we've even been tempted to give up. But we've also shared a lot of energy, a lot of laughs, and a lot of love. All in all, it's been a great adventure. But we couldn't have done it without a lot of help from our friends.

A very special thanks to:

- Steve for his unending patience and enduring support, his willingness to serve as a sounding board at ungodly hours, and, of course, for tending to four kids, three dogs, two cats, an aquarium full of fish, and a mouse during his wife's absence.

- Ryan, Peter, Mark, and Cara for believing in their mother and serving as the cutest guinea pigs imaginable.

- Shelly for serving as our conscience—scolding us for getting off track or thinking about giving up—and as a major source of inspiration—rooting us on, believing in our success.

- Our parents for believing that we're special, teaching us to work hard, and providing the kind of support that only a parent can give.

Our sincerest thanks to:

- Vicki for those long, hard hours—pulling our work together in those early days.

- Joe Martinelli who believed in us during those difficult days of doubt.

- Our colleagues for reviewing our work, providing moral support, and keeping us on our toes!

- The Technology Exchange Center for providing a learning laboratory and encouraging us to stretch our talents and grow.

TABLE OF CONTENTS

A WORD FROM THE AUTHORS...

The Quality Connection

We love to learn! When we were in college, both of us thought it would be great to be professional students, but we didn't think we could make a living doing this. So, one of us became a school teacher and the other became a parent. Both of these career paths enabled us to work in environments where we had to learn continuously. One of us had to stay just one step ahead of the kids, and the other had to be at least one step ahead of the class. About fifteen years into our chosen professions, we both experienced significant emotional events that threw us into a whole new world. Suddenly, we both found ourselves on the doorstep of the business world faced with a whole new cast of characters, a whole new vocabulary, and a host of new expectations. Surprisingly enough, though, we were both prepared for this transition. Why? Because we knew how to think. We knew how to transfer what we had learned in our past experiences. And, most importantly, we knew how to learn!

We soon realized that our strongest asset and greatest offering was our ability to teach, fueled by our keen desire to learn. For the past six years we have been working in corporate America helping businesses and industries throughout the United States adapt and put into practice the principles and concepts of quality thinking, or more commonly put, TQM. Total Quality Management is a philosophy that integrates a focus on the customer, a focus on process, and a focus on continuous learning.

Well, it didn't take us long to figure out that while teaching managers and employees to use the tools and skills of Total Quality Management, we were actually providing them with the tools and skills of continuous learning—helping them to continuously learn more about their customers, more about their work processes.

So now we get back to why this book? We believe that it's time to come full circle. The tools and skills of TQM include group problem-solving, process thinking, planning, data gathering and analysis, as well as listening, preventing and resolving conflict, and building cooperative relationships. As we watched managers and employees use these powerful techniques, we began to understand and recognize the incredible advantage that could be offered to teachers, parents, and students by bringing the lessons learned in business and industry to our schools and homes. We became determined to design and produce a vehicle that could transfer the knowledge and understanding we have gained back to our roots, back to teachers, parents, and children.

Just as the workforce of today are the students of yesterday, the kids of today are the workforce of tomorrow. And in this regard, just as our contemporary workforce has been shaped and influenced by our educational system, our educational system needs to be shaped, influenced, and guided by lessons learned in the working world.

In this book we will introduce you to many of the same principles, skills, and techniques that are making managers and employees more successful in today's unpredictable, challenging work place. Children well trained in the skills of continuous learning will be prepared to deal with and contribute to ever changing demands—becoming the powerful, productive, and confident workforce of tomorrow.

We want to prepare our youngsters now to become the "thinkers" who will lead us into the future. We want to prepare kids that want to, can, and do!

From the Field ...

One of the most fulfilling moments in our job is teaching adults—engineers, receptionists, accountants, or factory line-workers—to use these tools, learning to participate enthusiastically and with ease. But, perhaps one of our most vivid memories of success—and a source of inspiration for this book—is captured in the remarks of a young construction worker.

" Gee, if I had known about some of these things when I was in school, I think I could have been a good student."

Sure got to us! What about you?

PROCESS THINKING

Throughout this book we will refer to process thinking. But before we go any further, let's clarify what we mean when we say process. Simply put, a process is a series of related tasks, activities, or events that leads to a particular result. Learning to recognize that each activity is indeed part of a process seems easy enough, but how does this awareness of process increase our effectiveness? How does process awareness lead to process thinking?

Process thinking seems easy to adopt and even a natural way to think. But although perfectly logical, for most of us process thinking is a change in the way we have been trained to think, react, and do.

Learning to recognize activities and events as a process opens up an entirely new field of vision. Grades typically focus on the final product— test, paper, or project. Thinking process is a total switch and encourages students and teachers to look beyond the end result.

Grades of A, B, C, D, or F don't always tell the whole story—or reveal the process!

Peanuts © reprinted by permission of UFS, Inc.

INTRODUCTION

Try It, You'll Like It

We've always known that our future rests in our children...the future force. We are a nation dedicated to developing our youth. And, at the very heart of that effort are, of course, you—the teachers. As teachers your very profession is to develop capable kids—kids who want to, can, and do.

But, just like the leaders in business and industry, teachers everywhere are finding themselves trying to meet ever-changing needs and expectations while facing a declining economical environment. Budgets are cut, driving class-size up and reducing the funds for textbooks, computers, and extra-curricular activities. Yet even while faced with fewer resources and growing class sizes, teachers strive to expand their curriculum to prepare our youngsters for the increasingly complex demands of a high-technology world, while also trying to nurture their development in the skills and understanding they need to work together as people—self-esteem, communication, and conflict resolution.

Although this sounds like a lot to bite-off, teachers are doing it. Balancing the focus on back-to-the-basics and an emphasis on creativity and innovation, teachers are creating participative classrooms and integrating the principles of cooperative learning. So, while kids are mastering the academic and technical skills they need, they are also learning to work together—learning to work through and with the real-life issues of cultural diversity, bilingual work groups, and mixed abilities.

To sum it up, teachers are trying to do more with less. Trying to meet these complex and dynamic demands has caused teachers to re-think the way they manage their classrooms. Teachers are finding the contemporary educational methods of transmitting knowledge insufficient to prepare kids to deal with accelerating change. In order to develop capable kids, teachers have recognized that their approach must foster the type of learning that can initiate change, encourage diversity, and build a foundation for continuous, innovative learning.

Most teachers are finding it pretty difficult to create this type of environment and to implement the principles of interactive, innovative learning—especially when faced with budget cuts. Teachers are finding themselves dealing with larger classrooms with less help and fewer resources. So, although teachers know what they want to do, the "how to" seems less clear.

The tools we introduce in this book will help with the "how to." These tools will help you to create an environment which focuses on the learning process—helping kids to learn. Although some of the tools that we present might be new to you, others are not. What is new, however, is using these tools to facilitate interactive learning—learning initiated from within the learner.

This is not a textbook. We have tried to provide you with a handbook that you can use easily. We encourage you to pick and choose. These tools can be used separately or used together. But, however and whenever they are used, kids will experience a new dimension of success.

Before you jump in with both feet, we thought that you might like a brief overview of what you can expect to find in each chapter.

GETTING READY...CHAPTER 1

The tools introduced in Chapter 1 provide kids with opportunities to build individual skills enabling them to participate and contribute effectively in collaborative efforts—safely and comfortably. These tools provide communication channels that take the fear out of classroom participation, encouraging even the quietest student to express ideas freely.

Ground Rules
So what's so different—we've always had rules?

Rules are generally designed and dictated by the teacher. The process of creating shared ground rules with your kids is a new approach to establishing classroom behaviors.

Interviews and Introductions
Haven't we always started the year with some kind of introductions?

This interview and introduction process accomplishes much more than the typical introduction-type ice-breakers. Kids begin to recognize a sense of their own identity.

Expectations
Don't we always tell the kids our expectations?

Sharing your expectations with the class is an important step towards a successful year. But getting your kids to verbalize and share their expectations is the first step towards getting kids to take ownership of the learning process.

Issue Bin
What in the heck is an issue bin?

Introducing the class issue bin opens up communication and provides a safe way—for you and the kids—to capture and resolve issues.

Plus/Delta
Sounds like Greek to me!

The plus/delta chart is probably the simplest tool that we introduce, yet one of the most powerful. This simple tool provides you and your kids with a simple way to assess any lesson, any activity, any day.

TAPPING IN...CHAPTER 2

In Chapter 2 we introduce tools that develop levels of cognitive learning—perception, memory, analysis and judgement. These tools develop critical and analytical thinking. Kids learn a set of thinking skills which are applicable in a wide variety of circumstances, both in the classroom today and the work place tomorrow.

Brainstorming

We've always done brainstorming!

The guidelines introduced transform brainstorming sessions from harem scarem to productive learning experiences.

Affinity Diagram

What's an affinity?

This tool taps right and left brain thinking. The "right brain" generates lots of ideas; the "left brain" begins to analyze and organize.

Evaluation Criteria

What do we evaluate?

Anything and everything! Developing evaluation criteria helps kids make better decisions. And better yet, they learn to understand the decision-making process.

Light–Voting

Why?

Although lots of ideas can be fun to work with, how do you select just the right one? Light–voting gives everybody an equal voice, takes only a few minutes, and almost always guarantees a satisfied team.

Force Field Analysis

Is this out of Star Wars?

Nope. Force field analysis is another decision-making tool that gets kids to consider driving forces and restraining forces.

THINKING PROCESS...CHAPTER 3

These tools develop cognitive learning and can be used by individuals to plan, prepare, or think through projects, but they're also great for groups of kids that want to "think together."

Flowcharts

Follow the yellow brick road?

Why not? It gets you where you want to go. Flowcharts provide kids with a step-by-step picture of any process.

Interrelationship Diagram

Sounds psychological, is it?

Could be, but it usually isn't. This tool helps kids to understand and explore the tangled web of relationships.

Fishbone Diagram

Will this choke the kids?

On the contrary, using this fishbone frees kids up and evokes lots of ideas. The fishbone gets kids to explore the world of cause and effect.

Tree Diagram

Are we barking up the wrong tree?

No! This tool provides a structural approach to mapping-out and detailing projects.

Action Planning

Isn't that the teacher's job?

Action planning is everybody's job. This tool helps kids assume the responsibility of planning their projects and getting them done.

WORKING WITH DATA...CHAPTER 4

The tools in Chapter 4 introduce kids to the world of data. These tools will help kids gather, organize, and display data. As kids learn to make decisions based on facts, rather than hunches, they quickly discover the power of data.

Check Sheets
No, we're not talking about checkered bed sheets!

Check sheets are simple forms designed to help collect data easily.

Surveys
Ask me this, I'll tell you that!

With a few simple tips, surveys can be designed to gather the information you need. Designing surveys develops communication skills, planning skills, and even formatting skills.

Pareto Charts
Is that Italian?

Yep! Named after Vilfredo Pareto, this simple chart provides an at-a-glance snapshot of priorities.

Matrix Diagram
Sounds complex!

Not at all. This tool is simple to construct and easy to complete, yet provides incredible insight into the relationships between the items being compared.

Scatter Diagram
Who scatters?

Possibly the data points, but who knows? The shape or scatter of the data points tells if the factors are related, and if so, just how they influence each other.

Run Chart
Sounds physical. Is it?

Nope. Run charts are used to measure a process over time. The kids will learn valuable lessons and a new way of seeing things as they watch patterns develop.

WORKING TOGETHER...CHAPTER 5

In Chapter 5 we introduce effective communication as a team sport. Loaded with activities and techniques, this chapter provides the opportunity for kids to practice and master listening skills; learn to identify, prevent, and resolve conflict; and to begin working with their teachers and classmates to build stronger relationships based on open, honest communication.

The skills learned in this chapter are foundational, so in keeping with our "pick & choose" philosophy, be sure to tap into these activities when the time is right for you!

Working Together
Heigh ho, heigh ho, it's off to work we go...

You got it! The concepts introduced help kids to realize that good communication is the foundation for high-performance, effective learning, getting along with others, and building solid friendships.

Barriers To Good Listening
And the Walls of Jericho come tumbling down...

Identifying common listening barriers and learning to break them down are the first steps towards improving the communication process.

Learning to Listen
We have two ears, what's to learn?

Plenty! The skills introduced help kids to actively improve their ability to listen, understand, and retain verbal information.

Conflict in the Classroom
We can't have that!

Oh, but we do! Kids need to understand that conflict in the classroom is natural and inevitable. Conflicts range from simple spats to full blown fights. Identifying common sources of conflict is the first step in developing the skills to confront issues and resolve conflict.

Learning to Deal with Conflict
Who wants to do that?

Well, nobody likes conflict. But learning to handle conflicts effectively prevents lots of bruised feelings and paves the way for high performance.

The tools we introduce throughout this book will help you to improve the quality of the educational process in your classroom regardless of budget limitations and social complexities. With these tools, the thrust of your teaching role will be changed from content transmitter to facilitator of learning. You will find your kids taking on more and more responsibility for the learning process. And the real beauty is, they'll be doing so without being told. It's just an inherent part of the process. These "thinking" tools just naturally pull the kids in. They'll find learning irresistible as they energetically engage in the fun! And, although these tools develop rather sophisticated thought processes, they're simple to use. We think you'll enjoy using these in your classroom. So, try it, you'll like it!

CHAPTER 1

Getting Ready

> *"If you always do what you always did,*
> *you'll always get what you always got."*

Envision a classroom full of kids wildly raising their hands to give an answer or express an idea. Envision a classroom where teachers aren't policemen, but rather kids are policing themselves. Envision a classroom where everyone is quietly listening to the one kid who is speaking. That's what we see when we think about a classroom full of kids using the same skills and tools we've been using with their parents in corporate America. Having experienced the rush of power and energy that these skills and tools unleash, we delight in thinking about the tremendous growth and leaps in confidence the kids will experience. And, for that matter, the growth and increase in personal power you will experience.

It's not that we're tool happy. We don't believe that there is anything magical about any specific skill or tool. The magic is in the way these tools transform the ways in which we get things done—or better put, the way these tools improve the process!

The skills and tools that we are providing throughout this book are offering teachers, parents, and kids an opportunity to change their current paradigm and to expand their boundaries. Think about it: "if you always do what you always did, you'll always get what you always got."

We Can All Identify With the Problem

"Here is Edward Bear, coming downstairs now, bump, bump, bump, on the back of his head, behind Christopher Robin. It is, as far as he knows, the only way of coming downstairs, but sometimes, he feels that there really is another way... if only he could stop bumping for a moment and think of it."

Winnie the Pooh
A. A. Milne

There's always a better way!

These skills and tools will allow you to explore a different way of thinking and doing in a proven and effective way. Remember, managers and employees in business and industry have not only tried these tools and techniques and lived through it, but also are continuing to use them and are experiencing tremendous success.

But even businesses that have learned to integrate these tools into their daily work had to start at the beginning. People in the working world quickly realized that the first and most critical step is to create a climate of openness and trust. But just how do you accomplish that? Well, it doesn't happen overnight—or as Dr. Deming says, "It isn't instant pudding."

All of us would like to just agree to the importance of a trusting environment, snap our fingers, and make it happen. But it doesn't work that way. As in every organization, we need to break down current barriers, and gradually begin to build a foundation that supports open communication, honesty, and shared values.

In this chapter we intend to start with some basic tools for classroom management. And, much like these simple, but wise words: "We'll start at the very beginning, it's a very good place to start. When you learn to read you begin with A,B,C. When you learn to sing, it's do, re, mi." When you begin to create a class-wide safe zone, you begin with shared values and expectations, ground rules, and an issue bin!

The set of tools and techniques that we cover in this chapter can be considered the cornerstones. And indeed, these tools do provide the framework that will enable a foundation of trust to be built.

...or as Dr. Deming says, "It isn't instant pudding"

So, who's Dr. Deming? Dr. Deming is the quality mentor who not only helped Japan turn it's economy around, but also initiated the transformation of American Industry.

He is known for encouraging leaders in business and industry to be patient and persistent in their efforts to improve, reminding them that, "this isn't instant pudding!"

Think About It!

There are many occasions where "customized" ground rules come in handy.

Before launching into a special project or embarking on a field trip, have your class brainstorm guidelines and behaviors that will ensure a successful event!

Throughout this chapter we will refer to a comfortable climate, an open and trusting environment, and a safe zone. All of these concepts are synonymous and are fairly common terms. But, in order to assure that we're all thinking about the same thing, let's clarify what we mean when we say "safe zone."

A "safe zone" is just what it says: a place where individuals are safe. Safe implies there is no danger; one is free from risk, and can participate without fear. This is the climate we hope to establish. We want to free kids from inhibitions they have developed to keep themselves safe by creating an atmosphere that won't squash their egos or stifle creativity.

GROUND RULES

Purpose

Ground rules are the foundation for creating a safe zone. Ground rules are generated by the stakeholders in the class—that is, of course, the students and teachers. Ground rules are created by the students and teacher as a team—a team of individuals who will be working together and need to work together effectively towards a common purpose. And, you see, that's exactly what a class is—a team. We have not been conditioned to view a class full of kids with a teacher in that light. That's not our paradigm. But it can be.

Nobody can stand confusion, lack of discipline, or lack of direction—neither the teacher nor the students. There has to be order.

In traditional classroom management, the teacher has been expected to perform much like a boss or supervisor, the students much like subordinates. Rules are dictated to establish law and order, and the teacher's role has been to police and enforce them. The teacher's role as an enforcer somehow detracts from the primary role of educator, mentor, guide, and counselor.

Sample Ground Rules

- Start on time!
- Everyone joins in—everyone participates
- Share your ideas
- One speaker at a time
- Be a good listener
- Maintain each other's self-esteem
- Treat others the way you want to be treated
- Have fun!

Think Color

Blackboards are O.K., but flip charts and colored markers add a nice touch to the classroom.

And, whereas blackboards must be erased, flip charts can be saved and posted for visibility.

Traditional authoritarian classroom management sets up a win-lose environment. Law and order are based on position power as opposed to shared values and expectations. When you don't have shared values or a common vision of desired behaviors, trust can't exist. Nobody is safe. Both the student and teacher feel the need to be in control. The teacher must constantly monitor and direct. The students learn to be cautious and prudent, or in some cases—rebellious.

However, an open, participative environment does not suggest a free-for-all where everyone does whatever they want to do. We are not encouraging kids to adopt Br'er Rabbit's motto of "I do as I please, and I please me." Just the opposite. We are suggesting that the teachers, parents and children develop a set of ground rules together—ground rules that meet and respect the needs of everyone on the team.

Most conflicts or situations requiring disciplinary intervention do not occur because of lack of rules. Rules are everywhere. Most of these situations can be traced back to a lack of *shared understanding, shared agreement,* or *shared levels of commitment* to those rules. And, why wouldn't there be very different degrees of agreement and commitment to rules dictated by the teacher? Who owns those rules? The teacher. Who's expected to obey those rules? The kids.

Kids have been taught since toddlerhood to respond almost Pavlovian to certain rules—don't go in the street; don't touch; don't run in the house; don't chew gum at school. Why should they obey? Because the parent or teacher says so. Most kids don't think twice about the reasons behind these rules. Kids tend to see these rules as limitations hooked to punitive consequences rather than guidelines to support our values or protect our needs. In order to be meaningful, children must understand that rules are based on mutual values, mutual needs, and mutual respect.

The beauty of creating ground rules together is that everybody—teacher and student alike—contributes to their purpose and meaning. Ground rules are the foundation for creating a safe zone. Kids need to feel free to speak openly without fearing criticism and ridicule from their peers or disapproval from the teacher. Kids need to be able to express their ideas without being interrupted. And, as kids begin to feel freer and freer to contribute their thoughts, express their opinions, and share their concerns, you need to feel confident that you are still in control—a participative classroom does not imply a rudderless ship.

Creating shared ground rules establishes joint ownership, shared commitment, and a mutual responsibility to uphold them. Creating shared ground rules establishes an up-front, win-win agreement. Everyone knows and understands exactly what they expect of themselves and others. All cards are on the table. Everyone is responsible to keep the ground rules alive.

Process

Steps for Creating Shared Ground Rules

1. Clue the Class In
2. Clarify Roles
3. Consider Sample Ground Rules
4. Construct a Process
5. Conduct the Process
6. Carry them Out

Step 1 - Clue the Class In

- In the past, kids have not been involved in the process of generating classroom rules. You will need to tell them why you are doing this and encourage their active participation.

Step 2 - Clarify Roles

- Explain that in order to work together effectively you need to work as a team, sharing the responsibility to develop and maintain ground rules.
- Explain the concepts of "stakeholder" and "owner" in this process.

Hint: As a class, consider what being a stakeholder means to the teacher and to the student.

Step 3 - Consider Sample Ground Rules

- Post the sample ground rules we have provided. Have the kids talk about the examples and think about what kinds of behaviors or norms would help your class run well.

Hint: Start the kids off on a light, but thoughtful note by asking them to share some of their ground rules at home. Have them discuss which of these home rules work well for them, which ones don't, and why.

Step 4 - Construct a Process

- As a team, consider ways to get everybody's ideas and suggestions for possible ground rules out on the table.

Hint: Consider brainstorming. Refer to Chapter 2 for tips to using this technique.

- As a team, determine how you will take this large list of ideas and turn it into the set of ground rules you all want to live with.

Hint: Consider using some of the group decision-making processes explained in Chapter 2.

> ### *DEFINITION*
>
> #### Stakeholder
>
> *In business the terms "owner" or "stakeholders" refer to the individual(s) who have an interest or stake in the situation.*

Step 5 - Conduct the Process

- Review the process the class has decided to use.
- Work with the students to make sure everyone understands and agrees on the process.
- Do it and have fun!

Step 6 - Carry Them Out

- Remember the ground rules belong to everybody. Every member of the team—students and teacher—needs to support and use them.

Hint: This is a new concept for your kids. Once again remind them that your role is not to police them. Everyone is responsible for helping each other abide by the ground rules. Remind the kids to refer to the ground rules daily and to use them!

READY, SET, GO!

Ground Rules set the stage for teamwork. Teams that work well together create energy. This power is called synergy. Kids need to know about the power of synergy.

Consider posting the definition of synergy.

Synergy

When two or more kids work together towards a common goal, the results are greater than the sum of their individual efforts.

Facilitate a discussion about synergy by asking kids:

- What would Batman be without Robin?
- Can you imagine just one Ninja Turtle?
- What would Lucy do without Ethel?

Synergy can be both positive and negative. Help your kids explore the synergistic effects of the following:

- a gang
- a vigilante
- a clique
- the in-crowd

Have the kids discuss the differences between these groups and high performance teams like:

- the Lakers
- the Buffalo Bills
- a ballet troupe
- a band or orchestra

This type of discussion helps kids understand the importance of establishing shared values and ground rules.

OPTIONAL ACTIVITY

In order to create effective ground rules, you need to help the kids understand that rules support our values, protect our needs, and increase efficiency.

As you well know, you can talk until you are blue in the face about values and purpose, but kids need to learn through experience. So, before creating your ground rules, start off with this fun activity that initiates interactive participation and demonstrates the power of cooperation.

GROUP JUGGLING

Phase 1

1. Form teams of 8-10 kids.
2. Have each team form a circle with each kid facing the center.
3. Give a tennis ball to each team.
4. The kids pass the ball around the circle so that each person on the team touches the ball. However, the kids cannot pass the ball directly to the kid on his left or right.
5. Let the teams experiment until they develop a process in which the ball travels the complete circle without going directly from kid to kid.

Phase 2

1. Now that the teams have established a process, make things a little more difficult: "If you drop the ball, you must start over."
2. Continue to increase the difficulty. Give each team two more balls to work with.
3. To make matters even more difficult, have each team time their process and strive for better and better times per cycle.

Hint: Let the kids do their own thing. Don't answer their questions or provide assistance.

After the kids have worked through this activity, you'll find they will be anxious to talk about their team's experience. Guide their discussion with the following questions:

- What made this hard?
- Was there any bickering or arguing in your team?
- Did everyone on your team enjoy this? Why or why not?
- What did your team do to get better?

After some discussion, ask what rules could have been set-up first to make the activity easier or more fun. Record their answers on a flip chart or blackboard. Use this list of rules to transition into a discussion about rules that would help the class have more fun and run more smoothly.

Creating class ground rules together is a fun and meaningful experience—allowing many thoughts and feelings to get out in the open. This type of open and reflective sharing is the first step towards creating a safe and open environment. When kids recognize that the needs of others—both those of the other students and the teacher—are pretty much the same as their own, they quickly see that these ground rules aren't arbitrary rules for rules sake, but rather a pact between them, ensuring mutual respect and consideration.

The next technique, Interviews and Introductions, is another tool that helps break down the barriers that creep up between kids, as well as between students and teachers. The interview and introduction process provides the opportunity for kids to get to know each other in a way that includes everyone—and in a way that allows each kid to share a little bit more than they do on the playground or in the hallways. Although interviews and introductions are an excellent way to break the ice in the beginning of the year or term, this activity can be done at any time.

NOTES

INTERVIEWS AND INTRODUCTIONS

Purpose

Interviews and introductions continue the teambuilding process—serving many purposes. At first glance, the purpose of the interview process is simply getting kids up on their feet and introduced to the class. However, looking beyond the immediate lessons of interviewing, being interviewed, introducing, and being introduced—and even beyond the benefits of the class getting a feel for who's in the room—far greater values begin to emerge.

Kids begin to recognize a sense of their own identity. They begin to see who they are in their own eyes, what they choose to share, and how that message is interpreted and conveyed through their partner—and then received by their class.

On the flip side, kids have the chance to experience their partner's world, and begin to recognize that their responsibility is not only to portray their partner accurately and adequately, but also to help establish their partner's place in the group.

Interview questions should be thought provoking, challenging and fun. Some questions are more appropriate for a team just forming, and others lend themselves to a more familiar group. Look at the sample questions we have provided. We encourage you to mix, match, and make-up your own.

KICK THINGS OFF RIGHT

Do a little up-front work! Preparing the kids will help them get the most out of the interview session. Following is a great technique to use for this activity.

Purpose and Desired Outcomes

Purpose and desired outcomes are much the same as learning objectives, but they are geared more to share with the group. The purpose statement clearly states "why we are doing this." The desired outcomes states "what we hope to accomplish."

Writing the purpose, desired outcomes, and process on a flip chart posted for the kids to see is a great way to prepare kids for any task or activity. And better yet, kids not only know what they're going to do, why and how, they also begin to understand the planning and reasoning behind activities.

> **Purpose:**
> *To get to know your classmates*
>
> **Desired Outcomes**
> *Knowing who we are as a group*
>
> *Knowing your partner*
>
> *Knowing who you are and why you are special*

Sample Interview Questions

1. What is your first name or favorite nickname?
2. Where were you born?
3. Do you have any brothers or sisters? Pets?
4. What are your hobbies?
5. What do you like best/least about school?
6. How many languages do you speak?
7. Who is your favorite star? (t.v., movies, sports...)
8. What do you like to do when you are just kicking back?
   (read, listen to music, walk, climb a tree, just think…)
9. What are your immediate goals? *(win a soccer game, pass a test, do lunch…)*
10. What are your long term goals? *(become a marine biologist, travel through Europe, write a novel, win the lottery…)*

Process

Steps for Conducting Interviews and Introductions

1. Clue the Class In
2. Select Interview Questions
3. Conduct the Interviews
4. Share Introductions
5. Share Lessons Learned

Step 1 - Clue the Class In

- Let the kids know why you are doing this.
- Write the purpose, desired outcomes, and process on a prepared flip chart.
- Post for the class to see.

Step 2 - Select Interview Questions

- Select five to ten interview questions and write them on a flip chart.
- Post for the class to see.

Step 3 - Conduct the Interviews

- Encourage the kids to pick a person in the room who they don't usually hang-out with and don't know as well.
- Have each pair select three or four of the questions from the list you provided.
- Have them write down the information/data they gather.
- Tell them that they have 5-10 minutes to interview their partner.
- Let the kids know when to switch to the second interview.

Hint: Let the kids know that you are a member of the team, too, and will need a partner. Join in and have fun! Kids want to know who you are, too.

Step 4- Share Introductions

- Have the kids introduce their partners to the group.

Hint: You might want to start the process—lead by example. Remember, relax and have fun!

Hint: Consider recording key facts about each kid as they are presented. Catch key comments on flip charts or butcher paper and post around the room. Kids enjoy being able to read clips about themselves and their friends.

Step 5 - Share Lessons Learned

- At this stage, getting to know the different members of the class is the primary objective. However, kids learn a lot about themselves during this process.
- Ask the kids if they would like to share some of the new things they learned about themselves as a result of this activity.

Hint: Examples of what kids might say include:
- I wasn't afraid to get in front of the class.
- It was fun being introduced.
- I was really nervous.
- It was fun hearing about...

The interview and introduction activity is a process within itself, but the benefits gained fit within a much broader context. The individual insights gained by each student and the familiarity achieved within the group are incremental steps in the process of personal development, as well as in the process of team growth. This activity helps to build self-awareness and begins to build a climate in which individual differences are accepted, not ridiculed.

As you close this activity, expand their understanding by introducing the way in which the interview and introduction process is a part of the larger processes of personal growth and team development.

NOTES

CAPTURING EXPECTATIONS

Purpose

Not only do students need to know who they are and who they're working with, they also need to understand your expectations as well as their own. Whether you're beginning a new school year, a new semester, or simply introducing a new project or activity, breaking new ground is a challenge. Capturing expectations is a way to focus your students' energy as you work together as a team to verbalize and define goals, objectives, desires, and hopes.

Expressing and recording the expectations of each member of the class—teacher and kids alike—contribute to the team building process. This activity enables the kids to recognize that as individuals we all come into a situation with expectations, and that these expectations can be very different.

Some expectations are attainable, some are worth reaching for, some are unrealistic, some out of our control, and some even at cross-purposes. But whether simple or totally outrageous, identifying and sharing our expectations is an important step in the team building process.

We encourage you to let the kids freely express their expectations. You will probably find yourself wanting to guide, prompt, and even influence the direction or context of the kids' responses. Instead, actively participate as part of the team, sharing your ideas freely.

You will find that the shared ideas not only provide insight into the dynamics of your class, but also into the individual values and focus of each student.

Great Expectations

-What do you expect to learn this year in school?
-What do you expect to accomplish on this project?
-What do you expect from me?
-What do you expect to gain from joining the drama club?
-What do you expect from each other?
-What do you expect to be when you grow up?

Process

Steps for Capturing Expectations

1. Clue the Class In
2. Brainstorm Expectations
3. Clarify Expectations
4. Expectations—Next Steps

Step 1 - Clue the Class In

- Kick this activity off by introducing the concept of expectations.
- Write the definition of the word " expectation" on a flip chart.

Expectation: A hope, desire, or goal that could be fulfilled in this setting or situation.

Step 2- Brainstorm Expectations

- Introduce "Brainstorming" to your class.
- Post the brainstorming rules at the front of the class.
- Using the brainstorming technique, have the kids generate a list of their expectations.
- Record their responses on a flip chart.

Hint: Remember you are a member of the team: share your expectations, too!

- After the energy of the group seems to ebb, allow the kids five minutes of quiet time to think of other expectations they might have.
- Have the kids share any additional expectations.

Step 3 - Clarify Expectations

- As a group, you will first need to clarify the expressed expectations. Ask the kids if any of the responses are unclear and require further explanation. You might want to combine or eliminate duplicates.

Step 4 - Expectations—Next Steps

- Tell the kids that they are free to add expectations to the list at any time. Inform them that you will be thinking about how to address these expectations and hope that they will provide feedback.

Although the expectations activity is a valuable process within itself, it proves to be a part of the even larger process of visioning. Recognizing, verbalizing, and envisioning expectations is a first step in learning to create success.

Successful individuals are those that have visions of their future. Kids can learn to view their future as beginning now.

NOTES

Don't Get Confused

Expectations exist—you can count on it! Whether they're conscious or subconscious, spoken or unspoken, expectations can lurk in the background hoping to be met, quietly challenging your ability to perform. Or, they can be up-front and out in the open for clarification, discusssion, and negotiation.

So, don't get confused about the purpose and intent of capturing expectations! You're not promising that you can meet all expectations. You're not setting yourself up for the impossible. You are, however, trying to get everyone to tap into their hopes—what they consider probable or even take for granted. Yep! You're getting everything out in the open so that—as a team— you can determine the likelihood and probability of meeting the targeted goals.

Sample Issue Bin

- Some kids have computers at home, some don't.

- We need more parent participation.

- Can we build-in more quiet time at school to do our work instead of taking it home?

- Can we have more field trips?

ISSUE BIN

Purpose

The issue bin is a very simple tool—easy to construct and easy to use. In fact, an issue bin at first glance is merely a piece of butcher paper, a piece of flip chart paper, or a space reserved on the blackboard entitled "Issue Bin." But the issue bin—in all its simplicity—is an incredibly powerful tool.

The issue bin is a method that you can use in your classroom to:
- capture ideas or challenging questions that deserve further discussion or investigation at a later or more appropriate time.
- capture concerns or issues that pop-up in the class.
- capture ideas and suggestions.

The issue bin is yet another tool that provides an effective process that allows everyone—students and teachers—to get all the cards on the table. The issue bin process is a vehicle that opens and channels communication in a constructive way.

A Process to Deal With Issues

Select a volunteer to take ownership of an issue. Ownership means:

- The student reminds the class the issue is still active.
- The student tries to resolve the issue by working with his peers, teacher, or parent.

The student periodically provides status reports on progress towards resolving the issue.

Process

Steps for Creating and Using an Issue Bin

1. Clue the Class In
2. Post the Issue Bin
3. Construct a Process
4. Review and Update

Step 1 - Clue the Class In

- Explain the purpose of the issue bin.

Hint: Talk with kids about what types of ideas or concerns might be recorded in the issue bin.

Step 2 - Post the Issue Bin

- As a class, decide the best location to post the issue bin.

Step 3 - Construct a Process

- As a class, determine how issue bin items will be recorded.
- Consider items that pop-up during class discussions or activities.
- Consider issues or concerns that individuals want to record anonymously.

Step 4 - Review and Update

- Review and update the issue bin regularly.
- Check-off and delete items that have been dealt with.
- Determine a process for addressing and dealing with live issues, unanswered questions, or suggestions to be considered.

Think About It!

Construct a plus/delta as you grade a report, test, or project. Hand this back with the final grade.

This simple process would provide a student with a better understanding of what they did well and what they could improve!

PLUS/DELTA

Purpose

The plus/delta is another very simple technique that unfolds a process of openly sharing ideas. Simple to construct and simple to use, the plus/delta process only takes five to ten minutes and always triggers the active participation of everyone in the class.

The purpose of the plus/delta is to have everyone consider the pluses—or what went well, and the deltas—what could we change to improve the process. And, whether used at the end of the day, the end of the week, the end of the year, or to close out a project, the plus/delta is an effective evaluative device that once again opens communication and taps the energy of the entire class.

Process

Steps for Creating and Using Plus/Delta

1. Clue the Class In
2. Construct the Plus/Delta Chart
3. Conduct the Process
4. Continuously Improve ...

Step 1 -Clue the Class In

- Explain the purpose of the plus/delta process.

Step 2 -Construct the Plus/Delta Chart

- On a flip chart, or on the blackboard, write the symbols +/∆.

Step 3 -Conduct the Process

- Ask the class to think about what worked well and what didn't work so well—that is, what could be changed to improve the process.
- Record their responses on the plus/delta chart in the appropriate column.

Hint: Have each contributor identify whether they consider their observation to be a plus or delta. Interestingly enough, what some individuals consider a plus, others might consider a delta and vice-versa. In this case, record the comment in both columns.

Hint: When learning to use this tool, you will probably want to lead the session and to serve as the recorder. But as your class gets comfortable and proficient with this process, have students volunteer to lead the session and record.

Step 4 -Continuously Improve

- Consider the information you have captured on the plus/delta chart. The items on the plus side were considered helpful and effective. Think about what made these items successful. This feedback can help you when planning other activities.
- The items captured on the delta side should be considered opportunities for improvement.

Hint: Some of the items can probably be addressed or improved simply and immediately. To assure the kids that they are being heard, we suggest that you make the suggested changes as soon as possible.

Hint: For the items that need more thought, consider having some of the kids work with you as a team to brainstorm possible solutions or alternatives.

TRY IT

"A plus/delta is a great way to close the day, close the week, or close a project. What went well? What didn't?"

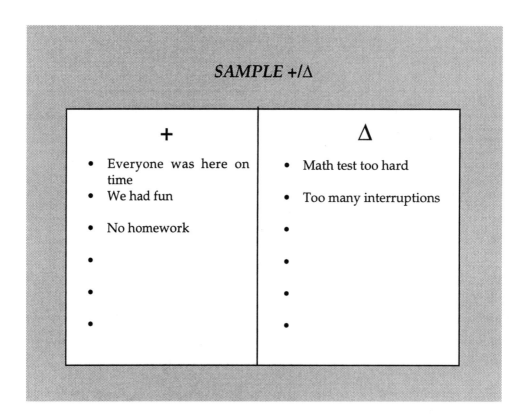

SAMPLE +/Δ

+	**Δ**
• Everyone was here on time	• Math test too hard
• We had fun	• Too many interruptions
• No homework	

TIPS

- Don't evaluate, judge, or defend responses.
- Record every response offered.
- Work on the deltas.

Summary

The tools and techniques we have introduced in this chapter work well together to build and sustain an open and trusting environment—an environment that engages the energy of every member of the class. By tapping into the energy of each and every individual, this process very naturally leads to the realization that creating and maintaining an effective, high-performance classroom is the responsibility of the entire team—students and teachers alike. Kids quickly realize that their cooperation and efforts are needed—not merely demanded. They realize that the classroom is theirs. They develop a sense of pride, ownership, and the desire to make things work. Kids begin to feel aligned with you as the teacher—recognizing that you are all part of the same team.

This new way of approaching classroom management—engaging the kids' support— frees you up from the role of traffic cop and enforcer, and allows you to dedicate more time to teach, counsel, and guide your kids through the educational process.

Parents are an important part of the educational process. You will find it helpful to clue your parents in and involve them in this new approach. They, too, will find these tools and techniques fun and effective. They will probably see applications in their own homes. Think about the advantages of developing a common vocabulary between you, your students, and the parents.

Can you imagine kicking-off your back-to-school open house by asking your parents to brainstorm expectations for the coming year? Would it help to engage their energy—their support? Think about it!

CHAPTER 2

Tapping In

The first step in creating a high-performance classroom is indeed to create an open and trusting environment in which kids can actively participate to their full potential. A safe environment is the first step towards stripping away the fear and inhibitions that bog kids down and freeing them up to tap into their creative energy. The second step is to provide kids with a set of tools that can harness this unleashed energy!

In business and industry, leaders have identified planning, organizing, problem-solving and decision-making as the fundamental processes underlying every project, every task. And, of course, in order to plan, organize, solve problems, or make decisions effectively, successful individuals have found that they need to be able to generate ideas, identify critical elements, and utilize significant data.

Aren't these the same processes key to the success of students and teachers? Of course. Well, recognizing these fundamental processes as key to productivity, leaders have developed and learned to use tools that maximize their effectiveness and efficiency. In this chapter we introduce these very same tools and techniques. Not only will these tools continue to encourage kids to participate freely, they will also effectively focus their efforts and maximize their productivity. And, better yet—they're fun and easy!

The first set of tools that we introduce can be considered idea-generating techniques. These techniques serve to kick-off the process of innovative thinking and help kids tap into their data banks, dig out the facts they've learned, and explore the concepts they have been taught. These tools work great with the entire class and for group projects—encouraging everybody to participate, increasing the energy in the room, and fostering a sense of teamwork.

Safe environment
set of tools

And, although these planning tools are indeed great for collaborative thinking, they're also effective tools for individual studying. Writing papers and studying for tests can be overwhelming. Sitting in front of a blank sheet of paper with pen in hand can be frustrating for some, tedious for others, and down-right frightening for the rest of us. Kids will find that while some of these tools get their ideas out quickly and painlessly, others actually help them to begin to organize these thoughts and outline their projects.

The first technique, brainstorming, has been widely used and is probably somewhat familiar to you. But with some helpful hints and suggested guidelines, this simple process can be dramatically more productive. The second technique, the affinity diagram, is not as widely known. The affinity, simple to use, takes off where brainstorming leaves off—adding the dimension of quiet reflection and a built-in method of organization.

The next tools, evaluation criteria, light-voting, and force field analysis, help students to analyze and prioritize their ideas, focusing their creativity to make sound decisions and to continue towards their final product, their bottom-line results.

BRAINSTORMING

Purpose

Think of those kids who either raise their hands hesitantly or don't raise them at all because they're afraid to spit out the wrong answer. Think about the kids who are just too shy to speak up, or those overly conscientious kids who struggle to come up with a perfectly stated, totally complete answer. Think of the kids who don't study as hard and might not know as much as the next guy. And think of those gregarious youngsters who love to be heard.

Well, brainstorming is one of those tools that meets everybody's needs while accomplishing a lot. Brainstorming is fun, easy, and powerful. Brainstorming is a great way to get lots of ideas out in a short amount of time. Kids love it and feel free to contribute. Why? Because all ideas are good ideas. Everyone is successful, everyone is smart!

Brainstorming sessions are simple to conduct and require nothing but a few markers and some large sheets of paper. However, although the physical environment is simple enough to set up, creating the "mental" environment can be a challenge.

Brainstorming can be such a powerful, productive technique if you follow and adhere to a few guidelines. You need to remember that all ideas are good ideas! Help your class remember the most important rule of brainstorming: absolutely no evaluating or criticizing ideas. Keep those minds engaged and the ideas flowing! As the teacher, you can set the stage for success and lead by example.

Process

Steps for Brainstorming

1. Clue the Class In
2. Review the Rules for Brainstorming
3. Identify the Topic
4. State the Brainstorming Question to Kick Things Off
5. Record the Ideas
6. Facilitate the Process
7. Clarify for Understanding

Step 1 - Clue the Class In

- Introduce the tool.
- Let the kids know why you are doing this and explain the value of this process.
- Write the purpose, desired outcomes, and process on the blackboard or on a prepared flip chart.
- Post for the class to see.

Step 2 - Review the Rules for Brainstorming

- Everyone joins in.
- Don't pick at ideas. (Don't evaluate!)
- Come up with as many ideas as you can.
- Wait until later to talk about each idea.
- Piggyback on other ideas. (Add on to someone else's idea.)
- All ideas are good ideas.

Step 3 - Identify the Topic

- Give the kids enough background so they fully understand what you are looking for and why.

Step 4 - State the Brainstorming Question to Kick Things Off

- Phrase the brainstorming question so that it invites creative participation. Try to keep it open to a wide variety of ideas. For example, instead of saying "describe a bus," try "if you were to design the bus of the future, what would you include?" Follow-up with encouraging words like, "think big!"

Hint: Remember, all ideas are good ideas. It's especially important that while brainstorming, you—as the teacher—accept all ideas equally. There's plenty of time for discussion after the brainstorming session has finished.

Step 5 - Record the Ideas

- Record each idea on the blackboard or a flip chart. (A flip chart is preferable.)
- Try to capture the ideas exactly as they are stated. Don't rephrase the statement unless you clear it with the kids.

Step 6 - Facilitate the Process.

- Pace the group. Make sure everyone has a chance to contribute.
- Remind the kids to follow the brainstorming rules. Continue the process until all ideas are generated.

Hint: *Sometimes kids get stuck. Remind them to piggyback off other ideas. This should help to get everyone going again.*

Step 7 - Clarify for Understanding

- After the brainstorming process is over, have the kids review the list of ideas.
- Check to see if anyone has any questions. Ideas can be discussed, but not judged or eliminated from the list.

Option: *If everyone is not participating, try a structured brainstorming process. Go around the room and have each kid give one idea. Kids without an idea may pass.*

Repeat this process until all ideas have been given.

KIDS CAN HELP

Have one or two kids serve as recorders for the brainstorming session. Ask for a couple of volunteers, supply them with colored markers, and you're ready to go.

Initially you should probably still serve as facilitator to pace the flow of ideas and to ensure that the brainstorming rules are followed. But once you've tried a few sessions and your kids have the hang of it, let the kids facilitate!

RULES

- Everyone joins in

- Don't pick at other kids' ideas (don't evaluate!)

- Come up with as many ideas as you can

- Wait until later to talk about each idea

- Piggyback on other ideas

- All ideas are good ideas

KICKING OFF A TYPICAL BRAINSTORMING SESSION

"Why we should have field trips"

Purpose:
- To generate lots of ideas that show why field trips are valuable and important to learning.

Desired Outcomes:
- A better understanding of why we take field trips.

- A list of ideas to share with the principal, PTA, and our parents.

NOTES

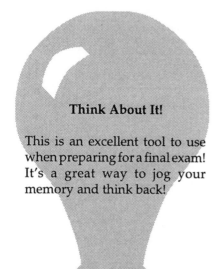

Think About It!

This is an excellent tool to use when preparing for a final exam! It's a great way to jog your memory and think back!

AFFINITY DIAGRAM

Purpose

The affinity diagram is a lot like brainstorming in that it gathers lots of ideas. But it takes kids one step further: it also serves to organize those ideas into natural groupings. Like brainstorming, the affinity is a very creative process, but whereas brainstorming is energetic and lively, the affinity is quieter, more reflective, more contemplative. Teachers and kids love using the affinity because it taps into both sides of their brain. The "right brain" generates lots of ideas; the "left brain" begins to analyze and organize.

The affinity is simple to construct and fun to put together. All you need is a large piece of butcher paper, flip charts, or even a blank wall for the backdrop, and self-stick notes and pens to capture ideas. The completed product proves to be an impressive conversation piece and adds to the ambience of any classroom!

Kids love to review the visible proof of their hard work and will spend lots of time discussing their ideas, learning from each other. They can also proudly share their hard work with visiting parents, principals, or even the teachers and kids from other classrooms.

Process

Steps for Constructing an Affinity Diagram

1. Clue the Class In
2. Set-up
3. Identify the Topic
4. Generate Ideas
5. Clarify for Understanding
6. Group Related Ideas
7. Create Headers

Step 1 - Clue the Class In

- Introduce the tool. Let the kids know why you are doing this and explain the value of this process.
- Write the purpose, desired outcomes, and process on the blackboard or on a prepared flip chart.
- Post for the class to see.

Step 2 - Set-Up

- You need a large space where note paper will stick. So, either select a blank wall, post a large piece of butcher paper, or use several sheets of flip chart paper.
- Divide packets of self-stick notes among the kids.
- Provide everyone with marker pens.

Step 3 - Identify the Topic

- Announce the topic you want the kids to work with. Phrase it in such a way that kids think comprehensively and creatively.

Step 4 - Generate Ideas

- Shout out your idea.
- Write it on note paper.
- Stick it on the wall.
- Absolutely no discussion!

Step 5 - Clarify for Understanding

- Have students discuss any ideas that are not really understood.

Step 6 - Group Related Ideas

- Absolutely no talking!
- Everybody attempts to re-arrange ideas according to natural relationships.
- Continue this process until everybody is satisfied with the emerging categories. (This takes time.)
- Discuss for understanding.
- Check for agreement.

Step 7 - Create Headers

- Determine logical titles for each category.
- Prepare header card for each category.

SAMPLE SEQUENCE...

Phase 1

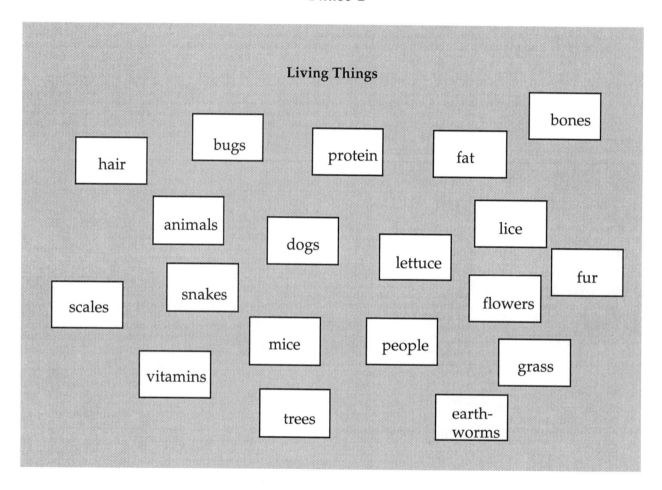

Living Things

bones

bugs

hair

protein

fat

animals

dogs

lice

lettuce

scales

snakes

fur

flowers

mice

people

vitamins

grass

trees

earth-worms

Random Placement

Phase 2

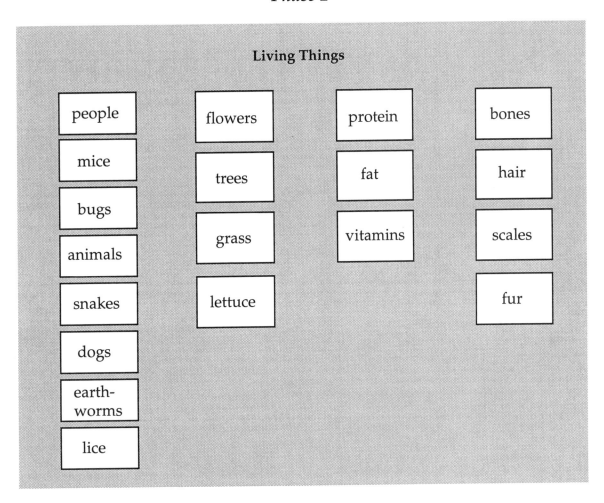

Living Things

people	flowers	protein	bones
mice	trees	fat	hair
bugs	grass	vitamins	scales
animals	lettuce		fur
snakes			
dogs			
earth-worms			
lice			

Natural Groupings

Phase 3

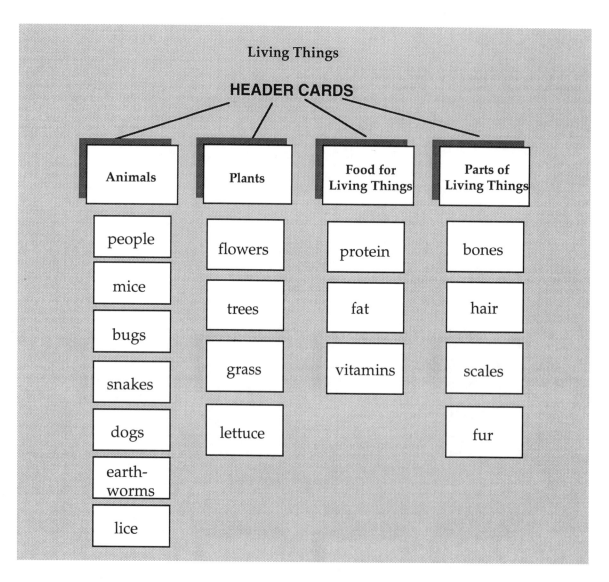

Titled Categories

NOTES

Think About It!

When you're faced with a tough decision, have your kids help you generate evaluation criteria. This brings them into the decision-making process and gains their support for the final decision.

EVALUATION CRITERIA

Purpose

After coming up with lots of ideas and even organizing them, kids still find themselves in situations where they can't quite decide what to do with them or how to proceed. For example, it's great to have lots of ideas for a group project, but how can a team of kids select just the right one for them? Or, after coming up with great ideas for a term paper, how can a kid focus his thoughts and determine how best to approach his chosen subject—what should be included, emphasized, or even left out?

Evaluation criteria are guidelines, rules, or tests by which kids can evaluate each idea or possibility. Having kids generate a list of written criteria helps them to understand the decision-making process. Some criteria might be pretty obvious, suggested or even required by you as the teacher. However, the kids will be fascinated to see that their own criteria usually contribute even more to the final selection process.

The process of generating evaluation criteria is the first step towards making thoughtful decisions. Criteria can then be backed up with data to take decision-making to an even higher plane—fact-based decisions—the key to quality.

Examples of Mandatory Criteria For a Group Project

- Involves everyone in the group
- Completed during class time
- Requires no outside help
- Does not require money

Process

Steps for Evaluation Criteria

1. Clue the Class In
2. Identify Mandatory Criteria
3. Brainstorm List of Criteria
4. Review the List to Prioritize
5. Apply the Criteria to Each Idea

Step 1- Clue the Class In

- Introduce the tool. Let the kids know why you are doing this and explain the value of this process.
- Write the purpose, desired outcomes, and process on the blackboard or on a prepared flip chart.
- Post for the class to see.

Step 2 - Identify Mandatory Criteria

- Give the kids your mandatory criteria. Explain to them why they are important. Explain to them that these criteria have to be met. Offer your reasons or rationale if appropriate.

Hint: For example, if when assigning a group project the project has to focus on a particular unit of study; or if you need to stay local and within a certain budget when planning a field trip.

Step 3- Brainstorm List of Criteria

- Start the brainstorming with a question like "What qualities would a great project have?" or, "What elements would an A+ paper include?"

Step 4- Review the List

- Have students review the list and check for understanding.
- Have students eliminate duplicates and combine similarities.
- Have students divide the list into two categories: Nice to have/have to have.
- Check for agreement.

Step 5 - Apply the Criteria to Each Idea

- Help the kids to use these criteria to evaluate their list of ideas or options.

Think About It!

Try using evaluation criteria and light-voting together. Evaluation criteria help narrow the choice and light-voting gets you to the final decision. This dynamite combination takes decision-making out of the win-lose mode and builds team consensus.

Everyone participates, everyone wins!

LIGHT-VOTING

Purpose

Group projects can be fun and exciting. They put kids in a situation where teamwork and cooperation are vital. But, although lots of ideas can be fun to work with, trying to select just the right "one" is tough for a group of kids. Everyone seems to have a favorite. How can a group of energetic kids select just one project and still come out with everybody happy? Sounds close to impossible, but it's not. Light-voting gives everybody an equal voice, is easy to use, takes only a few minutes, and almost always guarantees a satisfied team!

Light-voting helps move the decision-making process along. This technique enables the kids to check-in and determine where their team stands. When used in tandem with evaluation criteria, the kids will have a set of guidelines to help them cast their votes.

Light-voting is oftentimes one of the latter steps of the decision-making process. However, it is important to note that the word "light" is significant. The results of light-voting aren't necessarily the final decree, but rather one more piece of data to help kids make a thoughtful decision that the whole team is willing to support.

TOPIC \ STUDENT	1	2	3	4	5	SUM
ZOO	3	1	0	3	3	10
MUSEUM	1	3	1	2	1	8
FARM	0	0	3	1	0	4
EGG RANCH	0	0	0	0	2	2
VETERINARIAN	2	2	2	0	0	6
SUMS	6	6	6	6	6	30

Process

1. Clue the Class In
2. Determine Number of Votes
3. Post List of Ideas
4. Cast Votes
5. Tally Results
6. Discuss Results

Step 1- Clue the Class In

- Introduce the tool. Let the kids know why you are doing this and explain the value of this process.
- Write the purpose, desired outcomes, and process on the blackboard or on a prepared flip chart.
- Post for the class to see.

Step 2 - Post List of Ideas

Step 3 - Determine Number of Votes

- Count the number of items on the list and divide by three. This will be the number of votes per kid.

Hint: *For example, if there are 12 items, $12 \div 3 = 4$. So, each kid can vote for 4 items.*

Step 4- Cast Votes

- Each kid should quietly determine which items are most important and rank accordingly.

Hint:	*For example:*	
	First choice	*4 points*
	Second choice	*3 points*
	Third choice	*2 points*
	Fourth choice	*1 point*

- Each kid should post his number of points next to selected ideas.

Step 5 - Tally Votes

- Add up the number of votes per idea.
- Record on the flip chart or board.

Step 6 - Discuss Results

- Discuss the results and make sure everyone agrees to the final decision.

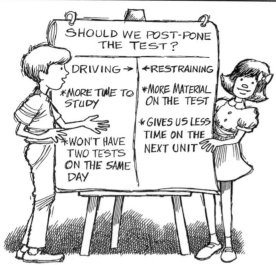

FORCE FIELD ANALYSIS

Purpose

Force field analysis (FFA) is a great tool to introduce when kids are working together and need to make a yes/no decision. This tool is also great when a kid is trying to make a personal decision. Should I go to this college? Should I join the debate team? Force field analysis helps kids develop their ability to think about the reasoning behind decisions as they consider the forces that either drive or block their goal. FFA gets the kids to think together about all the facets of their decision as they consider the "driving forces" that strengthen their cause, and the "restraining forces" that reduce their chance of success.

Force field analysis is simple to set up and requires no more than a writing utensil and space to record. However, although the technique is simple, the thought processes can be complex.

As kids verbalize and sort conflicting ideas, force field analysis transforms the pros and cons of ambivalence to a visual display of rational decision-making factors.

Driving Forces
Forces which move you toward your goal.
Restraining Forces
Forces which keep you from your goal.

Process

Steps for Conducting a Force Field Analysis

1. Clue the Class In
2. Prepare a Force Field Chart
3. Identify Driving and Restraining Forces
4. Review the Listed Forces
5. Develop a Plan

Step 1- Clue the Class In

- Introduce the tool. Let the kids know why you are doing this and explain the value of this process.
- Explain the concept of driving forces and restraining forces.
- Write the purpose, desired outcomes, and process on the blackboard or on a prepared flip chart.
- Post for the class to see.

Step 2 - Prepare a Force Field Chart

- Write the topic at the top of the chart and underline it.
- Draw a line down the center of the chart.
- Write "Driving Forces" on the left side beneath the topic heading and "Restraining Forces" on the right side.

Step 3 - Identify Driving and Restraining Forces

- Ask the kids to identify driving and restraining forces that affect the topic or decision.
- Record all forces on the appropriate side of the chart.

Step 4 - Review the Listed Forces

- As you review the listed forces, check for understanding.
- Have the kids brainstorm ideas for strengthening the driving forces and for reducing the restraining forces.

Step 5 - Develop a Plan

- Using this information, develop a plan for next steps.

IMAGINE THIS!

Each of these tools can indeed stand alone, but they're even more powerful when used in tandem. Imagine a teacher surrounded by thirty energetic third graders. The ultimate goal is to come up with team projects that thoroughly investigate and display anything and everything a third grade class should know about Thanksgiving.

Recognizing that the kids had already built a healthy reservoir of knowledge during previous years, this teacher decided to tap their knowledge banks by kicking things off with an affinity. After posting a large sheet of blank butcher paper, the kids were challenged with the header statement, "Thanksgiving: What's it all about?"

Armed with post-its and pens, the kids took the challenge. Although things started slowly, the kids soon found themselves filling the board with tidbits ranging from religious freedom, the Mayflower's voyage, Pilgrims, Indians, and the first feast, to contemporary traditions that highlighted the diverse cultures represented in the class.

Astonished at just how much they already knew, the kids were ready to organize the ideas into natural categories. Studying the categories initiated lots of meaningful discussion and set the stage for next steps.

After breaking the kids into teams, the teacher assigned a category from the affinty to each team. Each team then brainstormed possible projects. Of course the brainstormed lists contained lots of good ideas and generated lots of enthusiasm. But how could each team decide on just the right project? Well, instead of making a snap decision, some teams used force field analysis while others generated a list of evaluation criteria to help them make a thoughtful decision.

After allowing some discussion, the teacher taught the whole class how to light-vote. And, although each group did indeed need a little help from the teacher, every team ended up the proud owner of a project and all team members were ready to get started!

This scenario is easy to imagine—the giggles, the shouts of enthusiasm, the sophisticated dialogue of eight year-olds. Can you also imagine a high school class using an affinity to review a unit of World History in preparation for an exam? How about a group of seventh graders preparing a team report?

CHAPTER 3

Thinking Process

"A Thought is the Result of the Process of Thinking"

Without a doubt, teachers and kids alike will quickly see tangible results when using tools such as brainstorming, the affinity, and force field analysis. Decisions become better understood and gain more support when using evaluation criteria and light-voting. Undeniably, projects go smoother, reports become more thorough and better thought-out when using these tools.

But beyond the visible rewards, parents and teachers will observe tremendous growth in the way kids learn to think. And, better yet, the kids themselves will begin to see that they have learned to think and do in a whole new way. Kids will become aware that papers don't just happen overnight, that group projects involve planning, decision-making, and preparation. Kids will begin to see that a lot takes place from beginning to end, from conception through presentation. In other words, what they begin to see is "process."

The concepts and tools that we introduce in this chapter will take them one step further. The first step is indeed becoming aware of process or thinking process. The next step is learning how to define a process. Defining a process is key to effective planning, solving problems, or improving the way things currently get done.

Think about students who just can't figure out why they don't get better grades. Can you imagine how powerful it would be if they could define their current studying process? And, how about kids who have difficulty getting to school on time. Wouldn't it be an eye-opener to view their early morning process? These tools can also be used to improve your classroom process. Can you imagine having a class of kids working together to determine why they never seem to finish up before the bell rings? In these cases, defining the process would enable kids to identify problem areas in their current process and then to make necessary improvements.

Process tools are also great for planning. Think about how often kids overlook necessary steps and underestimate the time required to prepare a report or complete a project. How often do kids find themselves scrambling fast and furiously at the last minute, burning the midnight oil or sending good ole' Mom and Dad on an emergency run to purchase those "got-to-have right-now" supplies!

Well, in this chapter we will introduce the flowchart, the interrelationship diagram, the fishbone, the tree diagram, and action planning. These tools will channel kids' efforts and help them to visualize what really happens, what needs to happen, and who's involved.

And, once again, these tools will definitely help in turning-out better reports and better projects. But, the real beauty of using these tools is that kids will begin to focus on "how" the work gets done, not just the final product.

THINKING PROCESS!

So, what do we mean by "thinking process," and how do you do it? For that matter, why should you?

"Thinking process" is the ability to see things—events, activities, or tasks—with a systemic perspective. That is, learning to see how ideas, decisions, and activities impact each other.

DEFINITION

Process

A series of related tasks, activities, or events that leads to a particular result.

Learning to recognize activities and events as a process opens up an entirely new field of vision. The bad news is that "thinking process" is not always our first response. We usually want to jump right in and "do!"

The good news is that tools like the flowchart, fishbone, and interrelationship diagram help kids to start breaking down assignments or projects into related tasks and activities that work together towards the final goal.

A CLASS PROJECT IS A PROCESS

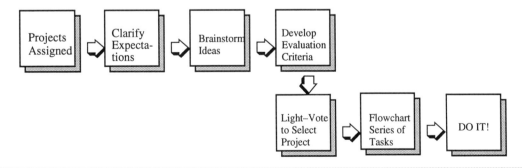

FLOWCHARTS

Purpose

Flowcharts are simple, easy to construct charts that show the major steps of a process. They provide kids with a step-by-step picture that can be used to plan stages of a project or to describe a current process. Flowcharts are great for sequencing a group project. Since a flowchart helps kids to see the whole project, they can pace themselves better, delegate tasks, and determine specific responsibilities. They also help kids determine which steps are more complex and might require more time or a little extra help.

Flowcharts can be simple or complex, broad-brush or detailed. To begin with, flowcharts can be as simple as listing the major steps. But, as the kids get more familiar with the symbols, they will be able to identify not only steps in the process, but also key players, decision points, necessary resources and timelines.

Creating flowcharts can be challenging, but fun. This is a great activity for a team of kids and initiates lots of insightful discussions. However, kids will also find that they'll like using them on their own to plan individual reports or other activities.

The flowchart as a final product is impressive and easy to read. Kids enjoy sharing their flowcharts with others and find that they serve as great visual aids when giving an oral report or group presentation.

Process

Steps for Flowcharting

1. Clue the Class In
2. Introduce the Symbols
3. Identify the Process
4. Identify Key Players
5. Brainstorm Major Steps
6. Sequence the Steps
7. Identify Key Considerations

Step 1 - Clue the Class In

- Introduce the tool.
- Let the kids know why you are doing this and explain the value of this process.
- Write the purpose, desired outcomes, and process on the blackboard or on a prepared flip chart.
- Post for the class to see.

Step 2 - Introduce the Symbols

- Draw flowchart symbols on the blackboard or on a prepared flip chart.
- Explain the use of each symbol and provide an example.

Hint: For example, the report symbol would be used for an outline, letter, math paper, or test.

Step 3 - Identify the Process

- Clearly state the process to be flowcharted.
- Identify the scope of the process—encourage kids to focus on the major steps and sub-steps, and not to get bogged down in detail.

Step 4 - Identify Key Players

- Brainstorm a list of people or groups of people who are directly involved in the process.
- Write the names of key players across the top of the worksheet.

Hint: Leave enough space so you have a column for quality issues.

Quality Issues: Those events, aspects, resources, or issues at each step that need to be considered to ensure a quality process or product.

Step 5 - Brainstorm Major Steps

- Encourage kids to anticipate or visualize what actually happens, what could happen, and what needs to happen.

Step 6 - Sequence the Steps

- Have kids determine the start point, choose the appropriate symbol, and draw on worksheet.
- Continue with each major step and sub-steps.
- Remind them to consider decision points.
- Encourage them not to get bogged down in detail when drawing their flowchart.

Option: Often it is useful to add a timeline column along the left margin of the paper.

Step 7 - Identify Quality Issues

- Review each step and identify necessary resources, barriers, and issues.
- Discuss steps to ensure the flowchart accurately represents the process.
- Remind the kids that this flowchart can and should be modified to accommodate change.

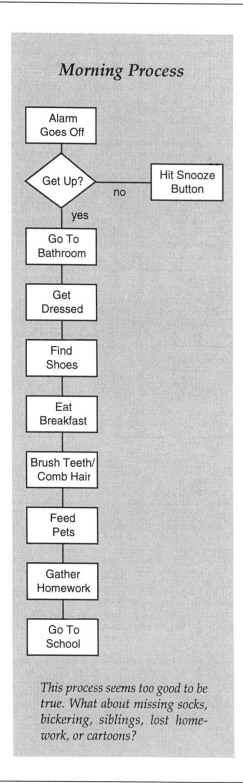

Morning Process

This process seems too good to be true. What about missing socks, bickering, siblings, lost homework, or cartoons?

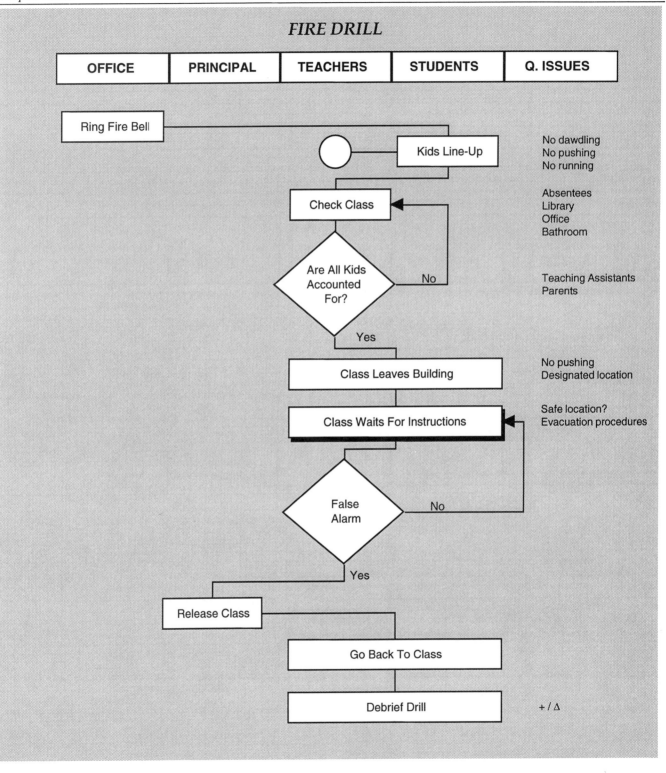

FIRE DRILL

| OFFICE | PRINCIPAL | TEACHERS | STUDENTS | Q. ISSUES |

Ring Fire Bell

Kids Line-Up

No dawdling
No pushing
No running

Check Class

Absentees
Library
Office
Bathroom

Are All Kids Accounted For?

No

Teaching Assistants
Parents

Yes

Class Leaves Building

No pushing
Designated location

Class Waits For Instructions

Safe location?
Evacuation procedures

False Alarm

No

Yes

Release Class

Go Back To Class

Debrief Drill

+ / Δ

Flowchart Symbols

Activity

Complex Activity
Involving More Than One
Task--A Process In Itself!

Group Meeting

Decision

Contribution

Report

Multiple Reports

The End!

Too Much Detail, or Not Enough Detail ?
That is the Question!

The kids will find when they first learn to flowchart they'll tend to get bogged down in details. A shadowbox is useful in helping kids to set aside the many substeps within a major step.

For example: If they were flowcharting their morning process, "alarm goes off'" could be seen as a major step, but "turn off alarm " is a detail that might not be necessary. Just as, "getting dressed" is probably a major step, "opening closet door, selecting shirt, or finding shoes" might not be necessary. However, these decisions need to be made by the individual because for some kids "finding shoes" might not be a major step. Other kids might find this to be a lengthy process.

IMPROVISE !

Butcher paper or flip charts are ideal because you can use colorful markers. However, if these are not available, you can just as easily use a blackboard.

Applications for teachers

Teachers can use flowcharts, too!

Try flowcharting these processes:

- Setting up the classroom
- Preparing a new unit
- Teaching a new unit
- Planning field trips
- Determining grades
- Planning a swim meet

INTERRELATIONSHIP DIAGRAM (ID)

Purpose

Sometimes when kids are planning a project or trying to solve a problem it's just not enough to create an explosion of ideas and then outline! Whereas the affinity helps kids to organize ideas into natural groupings, and a flowchart can provide linear direction, an interrelationship diagram helps kids to understand that events can be seen as a web of relationships. An interrelationship diagram is a creative process that maps out logical but not readily apparent links among related items. Thus, the interrelationship process can be thought of as an exercise in "creative logic."

The good news is, the interrelationship diagram is thought-provoking, challenging, and fun. The bad news is, it's not neat and tidy!

Using an ID is more than constructing a visual diagram; it is a journey of thoughts. And, although this particular diagram is not difficult to construct, it can be messy. As the kids wrestle with their ideas and try to identify what drives what, the pathways begin to criss-cross and maybe even cross-criss. Whatever!

Your class will have fun using this tool. Better yet, the resulting web of relationships is visual proof of their complex thoughts.

Process

Steps for Completing an Interrelationship Diagram

1. Clue the Class In
2. State Topic and Identify Major Categories
3. Set-up
4. Determine Interrelationships
5. Tally
6. Reproduce

Step 1 - Clue the Class In

- Introduce the tool.
- Let the kids know why you are doing this and explain the value of this process.
- Write the purpose, desired outcomes, and process on the blackboard or on a prepared flip chart.
- Post for the class to see.

Step 2 - State Topic and Identify Major Categories

- State the topic clearly. Talk about it briefly with the kids to make sure they understand.
- Identify the major categories and check for agreement.

Hint: Try not to use more than 6-8 categories. Any more than this can be hard to manage.

Step 3 - Set-Up

- Post large sheet of butcher paper or flip chart.
- Write name of topic at top of worksheet.
- Arrange names of major categories randomly in a circle around the worksheet. (Self-stick notes make ideal category cards.)

Step 4 - Determine Interrelationships

Select one category to begin with. Ask two-way questions to determine whether this category drives or is driven by each of the other categories.

For example:
Let's say your topic is "A Successful Class Project," and your categories are *resources*, *time*, *subject*, and *requirements*.

- Your first question could be, "Does *time* drive *resources* or do *resources* drive *time*?"
- You then proceed by comparing *time* in this way to each of the other categories. "Does *time* drive *requirements* or do *requirements* drive *time*?"
- You repeat this process with each category.
- Using arrows that point in one direction only, draw arrows coming from the drivers that point towards the categories which are effects.

Step 5 - Tally

- Count the number of arrows going away from the first category. Then count the number of arrows pointing towards this category.
- Write these numbers by the category name (number away/number towards).
- Tally each category.
- The category with the most arrows pointing away represents the main driver. Conversely, the category with the most arrows pointing towards it is the major effect.

Step 6 - Reproduce

- Since this gets messy, have one of the kids volunteer to draw a cleaned-up version.
- Post for the class to see.
- Make copies for the kids when possible.

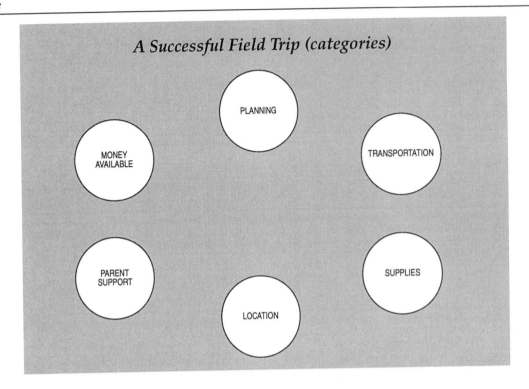

A Successful Field Trip (categories)

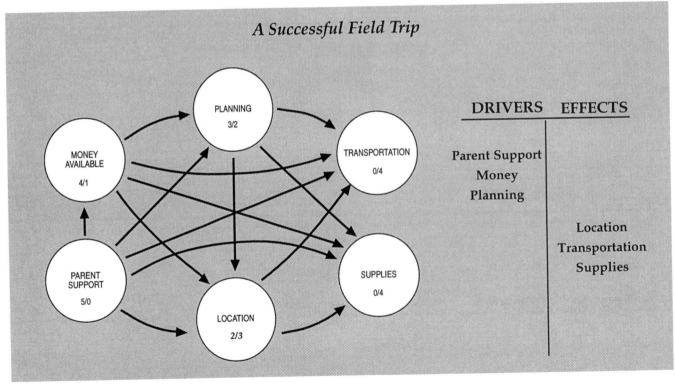

A Successful Field Trip

Summary

Although the interrelationship diagram can seem chaotic, this process is actually more reflective than some of the others. The insights gained from this exercise help kids understand the inter-relationships between the elements and activities involved in performing tasks or making decisions.

TRY IT!

Often times the major categories for an interrelationship diagram come from an affinity.

You can also use the major bones from a fishbone diagram.

Or, simply brainstorm the major categories.

FISHBONE DIAGRAM

Purpose

A rose by any other name is still a rose. Well, let's hope so! Dr. Ishikawa first introduced this tool as a cause and effect diagram. Consequently, many people now refer to it as an Ishikawa Diagram. However, it looks like the skeleton of a fish, so there's no doubt that kids would prefer to call it the fishbone diagram. So, fishbone it is.

As kids conduct the fishbone experience, they'll find themselves generating ideas focused to detail each "cause category." When the process is complete, they'll be amazed at the wealth of information displayed and grateful for the built-in organization.

And, you don't have to swallow the whole fish! After fleshing out each bone on the diagram, the kids only have to "bite-off what they can chew!" That is—they can tackle one bone at a time or even assign bones of information to sub-teams.

The fishbone is easy to construct and invites interactive participation. And, as many of the other tools, the fishbone, too, proves to be a great visual aid when preparing or presenting a group project.

Process

Steps for Completing a Fishbone Diagram

1. Clue the Class In
2. Set-up
3. Identify the Topic
4. Determine Categories
5. Identify Causes

Step 1 - Clue the Class In

- Introduce the tool.
- Let the kids know why you are doing this and explain the value of this process.
- Write the purpose, desired outcomes, and process on the blackboard or on a prepared flip chart.
- Post for the class to see.

Step 2 - Set-up

- Post large sheet of butcher paper or tape together pieces of flip chart paper. Allow ample space.
- Draw the fishbone chart.

Step 3 - Identify Topic

- Determine the topic, or the effect, that you are analyzing. Write the effect in the "head" of the fish.

Step 4 - Determine Categories

- Determine the major cause categories.
- Write the names of the categories on the major bones of the fish.

Hint: The general types of categories usually include such items as people, materials, methods, machinery, and environment.

Step 5 - Identify Causes

- Have the kids brainstorm the causes.
- As a cause is identified, determine which category or "bone" it belongs on.
- Record on appropriate bone.

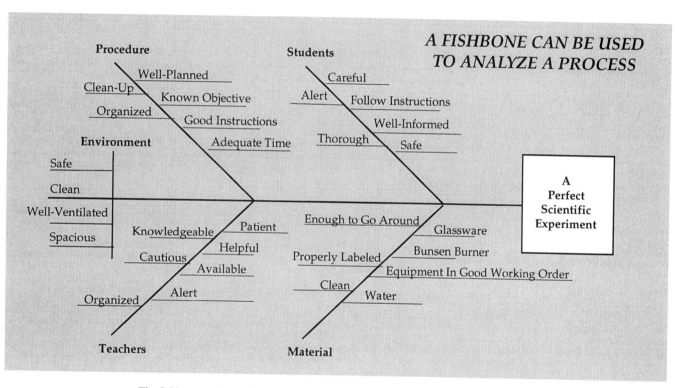

The fishbone can be used to analyze the cause and effect relationship in any situation.

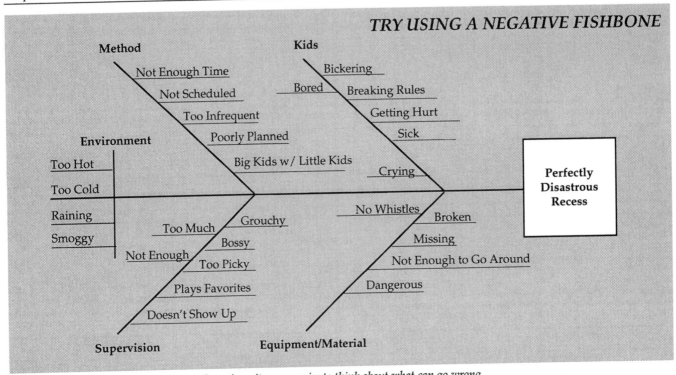

TRY USING A NEGATIVE FISHBONE

Method
- Not Enough Time
- Not Scheduled
- Too Infrequent
- Poorly Planned
- Big Kids w/ Little Kids

Environment
- Too Hot
- Too Cold
- Raining
- Smoggy

Kids
- Bickering
- Bored
- Breaking Rules
- Getting Hurt
- Sick
- Crying

Supervision
- Too Much
- Grouchy
- Bossy
- Not Enough
- Too Picky
- Plays Favorites
- Doesn't Show Up

Equipment/Material
- No Whistles
- Broken
- Missing
- Not Enough to Go Around
- Dangerous

Perfectly Disastrous Recess

Sometimes it seems easier to think about what can go wrong.

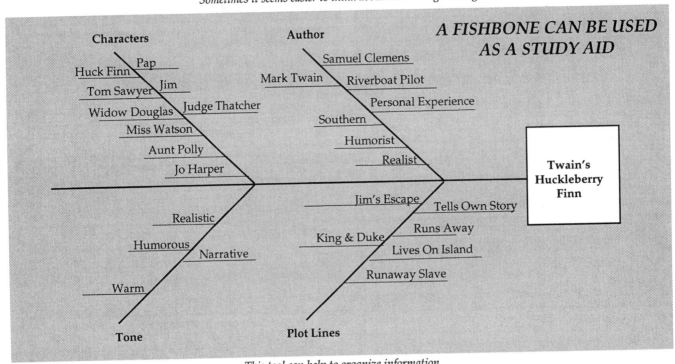

A FISHBONE CAN BE USED AS A STUDY AID

Characters
- Huck Finn
- Pap
- Tom Sawyer
- Jim
- Widow Douglas
- Judge Thatcher
- Miss Watson
- Aunt Polly
- Jo Harper

Author
- Samuel Clemens
- Mark Twain
- Riverboat Pilot
- Personal Experience
- Southern
- Humorist
- Realist

Tone
- Realistic
- Humorous
- Narrative
- Warm

Plot Lines
- Jim's Escape
- Tells Own Story
- King & Duke
- Runs Away
- Lives On Island
- Runaway Slave

Twain's Huckleberry Finn

This tool can help to organize information.

NOTES

TREE DIAGRAM

Purpose

This tool is sometimes called the systematic diagram because it provides such an organized, well-ordered, linear approach for mapping out and detailing projects. But we call it a tree diagram because it will remind you of a tree as the many branches break down and detail the full range of paths and tasks that need to be accomplished.

This tool develops planning and organizational skills as it helps kids to think ahead, forecast resources, and sequence events. Better yet, this tool enables kids to see tasks, activities, and events as related parts of a larger process.

The tree diagram is great to use when an assignment seems deceivingly simple. Your students' awareness of complexity will grow as they watch tasks explode into a practical level of detail. As kids continue to break down their goals, they will be amazed at just how much there is to do. They clearly see where their next steps will lead them.

Whereas brainstorming, the affinity, and the ID appear simple and chaotic—leading your kids through a maze of thoughts and relationships, the tree diagram is an exercise of structured logic. Who could ask for a more well-balanced approach to learning?

Process

Steps for Developing a Tree Diagram

1. Clue the Class In
2. Set-up
3. Identify Major Goal
4. Identify First Level Categories
5. Flesh Out Levels for Each Category
6. Review the Tree Diagram

Step 1 - Clue the Class In

- Introduce the tool.
- Let the kids know why you are doing this and explain the value of this process.
- Write the purpose, desired outcomes, and process on the blackboard or on a prepared flip chart.
- Post for the class to see.

Step 2 - Set-up

- Post large sheet of butcher paper or flip chart sheets.

Step 3 - Identify Major Goal

- Identify major goal or issue.
- Draw a rectangular box centered at the far left side of paper.
- State the goal or issue clearly and write it in box.

Step 4 - Identify First Level Categories

- Brainstorm the first level of categories.
- Clarify each suggested response.

Hint: *If you have constructed an affinity, you can probably use the header cards as the first level topics.*

- Check for agreement.
- Draw first level boxes and label.

Step 5 - Flesh Out Levels for Each Category

- Identify sub-topics, tasks, and activities.
  "What needs to happen?"
  "What do we need to do?"
- Record responses.
- Continue to explode each item until sufficient detail is provided or until you exhaust all possibilities.

Step 6 - Review Tree Diagram

- Look at each branch to determine completeness. Does the smallest level of detail lead to the successful accomplishment of the next highest level?
- Transfer tasks to an action plan.
- Assign responsibilities.
- Determine timelines.

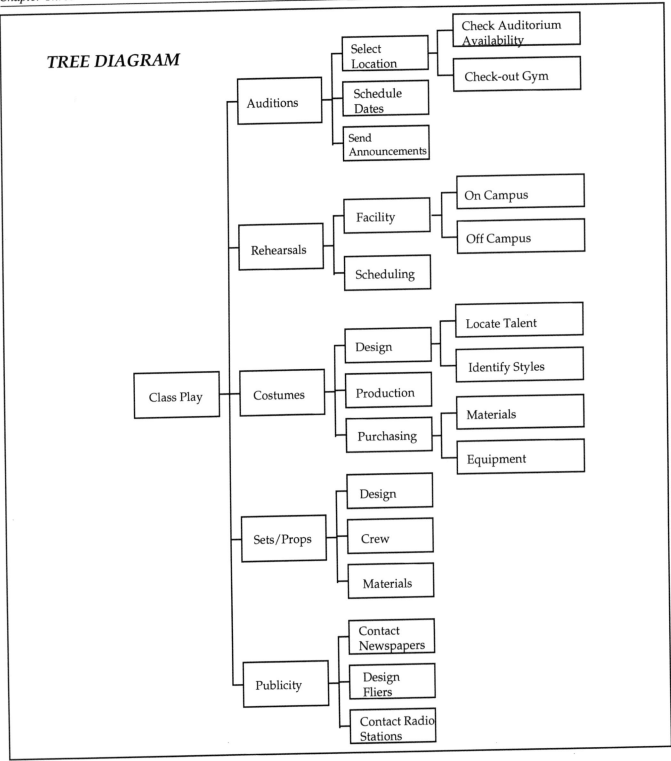

NOTES

ACTION PLANNING

Purpose

An action plan is where the rubber hits the road. An action plan helps kids put all those good ideas and planning efforts into motion, providing them with an effective method to monitor progress and ensure that each task gets done.

This tool is especially helpful with group projects as kids develop a written record identifying who does what, by when, and with whose help.

Action planning is a great process tool because it helps kids understand that a process begins with an idea, develops through analysis and planning, and is accomplished through a series of tasks and actions.

Action plans are not a one-shot effort used only to identify who does what. An action plan is like a project roadmap that needs to be reviewed periodically—checking progress, confirming target dates or re-adjusting to accommodate the unexpected.

Your class will hum when using this tool. Whether developed by individuals, teams, or an entire class, you'll find that projects run more smoothly when everyone knows "who's on first and what's on second…"

PROCESS

Steps for Action Planning

1. Clue the Class In
2. Set-up
3. Assign Tasks

Step 1 - Clue the Class In

- Introduce the tool.
- Let the kids know why you are doing this and explain the value of this process.
- Write the purpose, desired outcomes, and process on the blackboard or on a prepared flip chart.
- Post for the class to see.

Step 2 - Set-up

- Write the name of the project at the top of the worksheet.
- Divide worksheet into three columns.
- Label the columns, What , Who, and When.

Step 3 - Assign Tasks

- Identify tasks that need to be accomplished.
- Have kids volunteer for each task.
- Determine timelines.

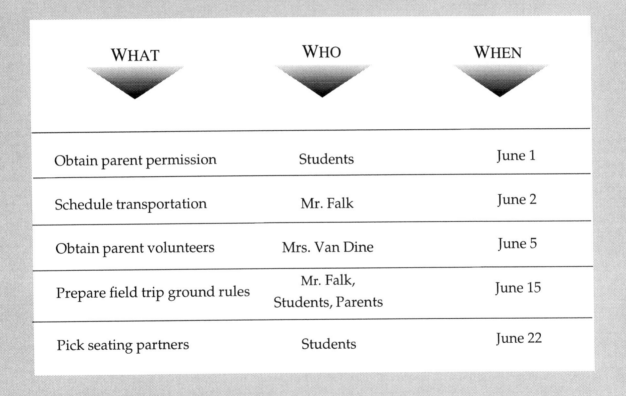

ACTION PLAN
Field Trip - Bronx Zoo
June 25th

WHAT	WHO	WHEN
Obtain parent permission	Students	June 1
Schedule transportation	Mr. Falk	June 2
Obtain parent volunteers	Mrs. Van Dine	June 5
Prepare field trip ground rules	Mr. Falk, Students, Parents	June 15
Pick seating partners	Students	June 22

An Action Plan provides kids with a visual reminder of the tasks they have committed to and helps the kids track progress.

IMAGINE THIS!

These tools can be used to plan a project or to improve an existing process. And, like we've said before, these tools can be used together—combining an affinity, flowchart, fishbone, and interrelationship diagram builds a thorough process to approach any endeavor.

Imagine a science teacher who is less than satisfied with the students' most recent attempts at an assigned experiment. Still frustrated with spills, broken glassware, minor injuries, and even burned hair, this teacher decided that rather than delivering an unwelcomed lecture on caution and proper procedure, he would launch the kids on a self-discovery improvement process.

To kick things off, the teacher had the kids flowchart the experimental process from the initial set-up to final reports. The kids were amazed at just how complex and involved the process actually was as they flowcharted each and every step, identified decision points, and determined quality issues.

After completing the flowchart and gaining a better understanding of their process, the kids then constructed a fishbone. They entitled the head of the fish "How to Conduct a Perfectly Disastrous Experiment."

Brainstorming the elements to fill each bone evoked not only lots of laughs, but also much insight into causes for error and mishaps. These two diagrams initiated a meaningful discussion where the students were able to talk about their frustrations, question their mistakes, and share lessons learned. The final step was to create an action plan that specified steps for improvement and ensured a more successful experience next time around!

This scenario portrays how a classroom of students could work together to improve a process. But, these tools can be used by individuals as well as groups. Can you imagine the powerful insight an individual student could gain if he were to flowchart his homework or study process? Could be an eye-opener!

WHAT WENT WRONG?

Could I improve my process?

CHAPTER 4

Working With Data

Learning to think "process" is at the very heart of Total Quality Management. Once the kids begin using tools like the flowchart and the fishbone to define and plan classroom or project processes, they'll be well on their way to thinking process. Being able to recognize, define, and plan processes prepares kids to think systemically, but they also need to work systematically. Big words, but what exactly do they mean?

Leaders in business and industry would probably sum it up in two words: the scientific approach. The scientific approach is simply a systematic way to learn and work. And it's important to note that the scientific approach is not limited to science projects. Kids can and should learn to think and work through any project or decision with logic and reasoning. The planning and process tools introduced in the previous chapters set kids up to work through processes in a logical, well-planned manner. However, by themselves, these tools aren't always enough.

Although flowcharting, analyzing cause and effect, and identifying interrelationships launches one well into the world of process or systems thinking, kids need to go one step further in order to fully understand any process or situation. They need to gather data! Kids need to learn to make decisions based on data rather than hunches. They need to look beyond and behind superficial symptoms and surface opinions. They need to dig for the root cause and seek out all pertinent information.

PDCA CYCLE
The Scientific Approach

Plan

- State the problem to be solved or identify the project.
- Clarify objectives and goals.
- Identify key players or team members.
- Plan activities.

Do

- Design appropriate tools.
- Do appropriate activities.

Check

- Check the progress against your goals and objectives.
- See if your plan is working.
- Identify and remove roadblocks.

Act

- Complete action.
- Document findings.
- Communicate results.

The set of tools we introduce in this chapter will help kids to gather, organize, and display data. Once again, not only will the kids have fun using the tools, they'll learn a lot and be proud of their work. Gathering data is quite a learning experience. Kids will be amazed at how their perspective changes as their knowledge base grows. As kids learn to use check sheets and develop surveys, they will find that gathering data can be a real adventure—much like a scavenger hunt.

And, after the kids have gathered data and begin to use tools like Pareto charts, run charts, or scatter diagrams to graph this information, they'll quickly learn to respect the power of data. These tools visually organize and display data so that kids—and their teachers—can readily size-up a situation, make decisions, and convey their conclusions to others.

PDCA CYCLE

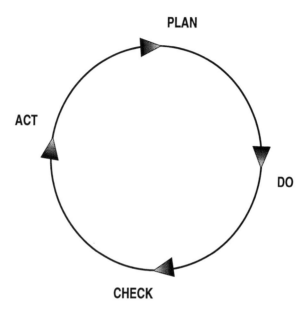

In the 1920s Dr. Shewhart of Bell Laboratories developed this simple model to help workers focus on process improvement. Wonderful in its simplicity, Shewhart presented the method scientists have used and found effective for centuries—but managed to do so in a simple model that we can follow to accomplish our goals.

Most kids—and adults—find themselves in a whirlwind of do-check-do-check-do-check -do, or even worse—a never ending series of do-do-do. . .

This model helps kids to focus on the process—the way work gets done—not just the final results.

Hint: *Consider having your kids construct a PDCA cycle that you can post in your room as a continuous memory jogger, reminding the kids that a complete, thorough process always begins with planning.*

GATHERING DATA

Once kids have identified a project or process, they need to determine the purpose or objective. Once this has been accomplished, they need to determine what kind of data is needed and then figure out how best to collect it. Check sheets and simple surveys are effective methods, easy to design, and fun to implement either as an individual or as a part of a team.

Check Sheets

Check sheets are used to indicate the frequency of an event or activity. The best check sheets are simple to use and visually display the data in a format that can reveal underlying patterns.

Check sheets often provide a snapshot of the process being studied.

Surveys

Kids will enjoy designing surveys as well as conducting them. And, both steps are lessons in themselves. Designing surveys requires lots of planning and provides a great use for some of the planning tools taught in Chapter 2.

Surveys are usually designed as questionnaires or interviews. They can be qualitative or quantitative—very detailed and specific or fairly general. But whatever, designing surveys develops creative skills, planning skills, communication skills, writing skills, and even formatting skills.

TIPS FOR DESIGNING DATA COLLECTION FORMS

Tips for Designing Check Sheets

1. Determine the types or categories of data to be collected.
2. Create a check sheet form. Be sure that the columns are clearly labeled and have enough room for check marks.
3. Collect data and record the number of occurrences.
4. If more than one kid is collecting data and more than one check sheet is used, transfer data to a cumulative check sheet.

Tips for Designing Surveys

1. Determine what questions this survey will answer.
2. Determine what depth of information is needed. (Is very detailed information needed or is broad, overall information sufficient?)
3. Determine whether the survey will be qualitative or quantitative.

   For example:

   > Qualitative surveys could rate responses with terms like poor, satisfactory, excellent. As well, qualitative surveys can ask open-ended questions. Quantitative surveys use terms like, "how often?" followed by a numerical scale.

4. If appropriate, select a rating scale.
5. Determine how the data collected will be analyzed. What tools can or should be used?

Process

Steps for Data Gathering

1. Clue the Class In
2. Select a Class Project
3. Develop Data Gathering Plan
4. Design the Tool
5. Collect Data

Step 1 - Clue the Class In

- Introduce the concept of the scientific approach. Talk to the kids about how to approach a problem or project using the PDCA Cycle.

Hint: Post the PDCA Cycle on a wall or draw it on a chalk board.

- Talk to the kids about the importance of using data to answer questions, solve problems, or present new ideas. Have the kids think about other people who use data in their jobs—doctors, detectives, lawyers...

Hint: Ask the kids if a doctor would prescribe medicine or perform surgery without gathering some data. What kind of data do doctors need? Help the kids recognize that doctors use all kinds of data, ranging from symptoms to x-rays to sophisticated lab tests.

Lead a discussion that helps the kids see that data gathering is a building process. You'll want your kids to see that the initial data—like symptoms—are important, but don't always get to the root cause. For example, a doctor wouldn't perform surgery or cast an arm without x-rays or lab tests; however, he wouldn't know which tests to run without knowing the symptoms!

Step 2 - Select a Class Project

- Tell the kids that you would like to plan a class project that will help them learn how to collect and analyze data. Provide some broad objectives. For example, think about improving a classroom process, improving a school-wide or community process, or focusing on a topic from your curriculum.

Option: Instead of doing this as an entire class, have the kids form teams with projects of their own.

- Use some of the tools from Chapter 2 to generate lots of ideas for a class project.
- Generate evaluation criteria and use light-voting to select your class project.
- Use the process tools in Chapter 3 to define the process being studied and to focus your efforts.

LATE HOMEWORK CHECK SHEET		
EXCUSES	FREQUENCY	TOTALS
Kid brother needed help with homework	√√√	3
Library research required extra time	√√	2
Mom had a baby	√	1
Lost assignment	√√√√	4
Did not know there was an assignment	√√√√√√√√√	9
Did not understand the assignment	√√√√√√√	7
Watched TV instead of doing homework	√√√√	4
Total		30

Step 3 - Develop Data Gathering Plan

- Have the kids determine what kinds of information they will need. The kids will quickly see that some of the information will be obtained through researching books or magazines, but other information will require data gathering.
- Review the check sheet and survey as data gathering options.
- Briefly introduce data analysis tools so the kids can see how they can evaluate and present the data they collect.
- Have the kids prepare a data gathering worksheet that answers the following questions:

  1. Why do you want this data?
  2. What could this data tell you?
  3. How will you collect this data?
  4. Who will collect this data?
  5. When will this data be collected? (What time period—from when to when?)
  6. What won't the data tell you?

- Have the kids prepare a data gathering action plan.

Step 4 - Design the Tools

- Provide the kids with the tips for creating check sheets or designing surveys.
- Remind the kids that surveys and check sheets are effective tools, but might not be appropriate for their data gathering plan. Encourage them to be creative and to design a data gathering worksheet that works best for them.
- Design the tool.

Step 5 - Collect Data

- Begin collecting data.

Remember! In the spirit of PDCA, be sure to have the kids check in periodically to see if the right data is being collected.

DON'T LET THE DATA FOOL YOU!

Check sheets provide data points...not the answer!

CLASSROOM DELAYS CHECK SHEET		
TYPES OF DELAYS	**FREQUENCY**	**TOTALS**
Kids Talking	√√√√√√√	7
Visitors coming into classroom	√√	2
Fire Drill	√	1
Teachers coming to class late	√√√√√	5
Students coming to class late	√√√√√	5
Misplaced materials	√√√√√√ √√√√√	12
Total (Time period: 7 days)		32

Challenge your kids to improve a classroom process. One of the first steps is to understand the causes of poor performance. A check sheet will help identify some of these causes and will clearly indicate the frequency of which they occur.

INJURIES ON THE PLAYGROUND OR IN THE CLASSROOM		
INJURY	**FREQUENCY**	**TOTALS**
Bruises	√√√√√√ √√√√√	12
Burns	√	1
Eye injuries	√	1
Head injuries		0
Scrapes/ abrasions	√√√√√√√√	8
Sprains	√√√	3
Broken bones	√√	2
Total (Time period: 6 months)		27

Don't let the data fool you! Just because an incident occurs most often doesn't necessarily mean that it's the one to work on first. Identify those that require immediate attention, those which are easily fixed, and those that will require further investigation.

SURVEYS CAN BE FUN!

HALLOWEEN CARNIVAL

Instructions: Please rate the following by checking the appropriate column or by filling in the appropriate blank.

QUESTION	☺ Great	☺ OK	☹ Poor
1 The game booths were			
2 The haunted house was			
3 The food served in the cafeteria was			
4 Service in the cafeteria was			
5 The costume parade was			
6 What was your favorite game?			_____
7 Did you participate in the costume parade?			_____
8 What was your favorite food at the carnival?			_____
9 Were the prices fair?			_____

ANALYZING DATA

After the kids feel that data collection is complete, they'll need to review their work to make sure they really do have all the necessary data. The next step is analysis.

The tools we introduce in this section will help the kids to organize, analyze, and display their data. These graphical tools are simple to construct and don't require a sophisticated statistical background. The kids will be amazed at how much they've learned about the process being studied. The depth of knowledge gained will boost self-confidence as kids proudly present their findings and make recommendations and decisions based on facts.

Pareto Chart

Pareto charts are probably the most simple data analysis tool. A Pareto chart is a series of vertical bars lined up in a descending order—from high to low— to reflect frequency, importance, or impact. Because of the descending order, Pareto charts quickly draw everyone's attention to the most important factor—providing an at-a-glance snapshot of priorities.

Matrix Diagram

Matrix diagrams organize data or pieces of information such as characteristics, requirements, or tasks into sets of items to be compared. The matrix diagram quickly reveals relationships between the items in each set. As well, a matrix diagram evaluates the strength of that relationship.

| **Common Cause** |
| Common Cause variation is a situation or event that occurs repeatedly. |
| **Special Cause** |
| Special Cause variation occurs sporadically or infrequently and might arise because of specific circumstances. |

Matrix diagrams add a valuable addition to the kids' tool kit. Simple to construct, they are a powerful tool because of their flexibility and diverse applications. First of all, kids will find the content they can choose for a matrix is limitless. Beyond that, they can even shape the format of their matrix to meet their needs.

Scatter Diagram

A scatter diagram plots two variables against each other and displays the relationship between them. The shape or scatter of the points tells you if the factors are related, and if so, just how they influence each other. If they are unrelated, the plots will be scattered randomly around the graph—like a shotgun blast. If the plots have a definite slope and appear to be grouped in a pattern, then a negative or positive relationship may exist—and you need to investigate!

Run Chart

Run charts are simple to construct and easy to read. Run charts are used to measure a process over time. Run charts, also called "time plots," are used to study data to reveal trends or patterns that occur during a period of time.

The kids will learn valuable lessons and a new way of seeing things as they watch patterns develop. But while kids watch a pattern develop, they will also identify data points that disrupt the pattern. That's how they'll begin to understand the concept of common cause/ special cause!

TOOLS FOR DATA ANALYSIS
Construction Tips

Pareto Chart

1. Construct a graph with a vertical and horizontal axis.
2. Label each axis.
3. Divide the vertical axis into even increments with the selected units of measure.
4. Include a title for each category being studied along the horizontal axis.
5. Plot the data as bars. Start with the largest category at the far left. Continue plotting data from the largest to smallest.

Loss of Class Work Time

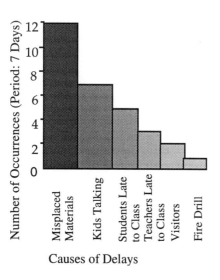

Late Homework

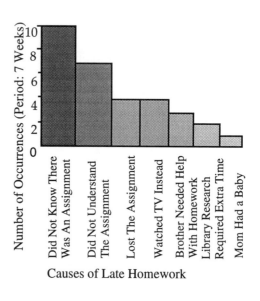

Note: The data from the earlier check sheets become more meaningful when displayed as Pareto Charts.

TOOLS FOR DATA ANALYSIS
Construction Tips

Matrix Diagram

1. Identify the sets of data to be compared.
2. Put the first set of items along the vertical axis. Put the second set of items along the horizontal axis.
3. Draw in grid lines.
4. Determine the symbols to be used to rate relationships. Provide a legend.

> *+ strong relationship*
> *O some relationship*
> *Δ no relationship*

5. Enter the appropriate symbols into each box.

CHOOSING A PROJECT THAT'S BEST FOR YOU

	Build a Replica of the Mayflower	Write a Story About a Pilgrim	Draw a Map that Shows the Mayflower's Journey	Write a Report on the Pilgrims' First Thanksgiving Dinner	Perform a Play About the Pilgrims' and Indians' First Encounter	Give an Oral Report on the Hardships Endured on the Mayflower
Reading Core Material	O	+	O	+	+	+
Doing Research	O	+	O	+	+	+
Art Work	+	Δ	+	Δ	O	Δ
Speaking in Front of the Class	Δ	Δ	Δ	Δ	+	+
Craft Skills	+	Δ	O	Δ	O	Δ
Art Supplies	+	Δ	O	Δ	O	Δ
Team Work	O	Δ	Δ	Δ	+	Δ
Writing	Δ	+	Δ	+	+	+

Legend: + strong relationship   O some relationship   Δ no relationship

TOOLS FOR DATA ANALYSIS
Construction Tips

Scatter Diagram

1. Construct a graph with a vertical and horizontal axis.
2. Label each axis.
3. Divide each axis into even increments with the selected units of measure.
4. Plot the data points.
5. Title the diagram.

Positive Correlation

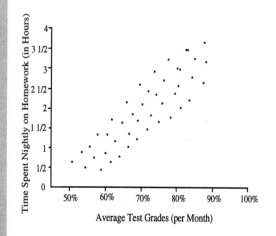

No Correlation

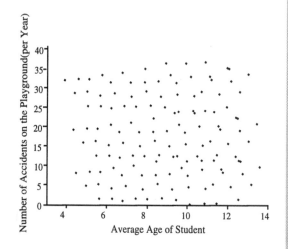

TOOLS FOR DATA ANALYSIS
Construction Tips

Run Chart

1. Construct a graph with a vertical and horizontal axis.
2. Label each axis.
3. Divide each axis into even increments with the selected units of measurement.
4. Plot the data points.
5. Title the diagram.

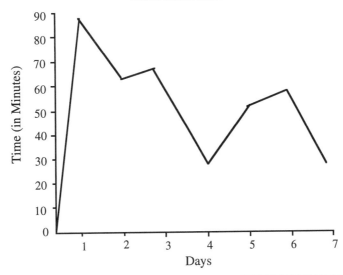

Class Time Lost

DATA SUMMARY SHEET			
DAY	**TYPE**	**TIME**	**TOTAL TIME LOST**
1	Kids Talking Misplaced Materials Fire Drill	25 45 20	90 Minutes
2	Teachers late Visitors Kids Talking	12 36 16	64 Minutes

Process

Steps for Data Analysis

1. Clue the Class In
2. Review the Data Analysis Tools
3. Select Appropriate Tools for Data Display
4. Graph Data
5. Analyze Data
6. Prepare Report
7. Present Results
8. Celebrate

Step 1 - Clue the Class In

- Initiate discussion on "Why Data?"
- Have the kids conduct a plus/delta on their data gathering experience.

Hint: Think Teamwork! Encourage kids to reflect on the whole experience, considering their team process as well as content.

Have kids report-out.

Hint: Listen closely to their report-outs. You'll undoubtedly gain tremendous insight into the team interactions, successess, lessons learned, and roadblocks encountered. This information will be valuable as you guide them through data analysis.

- Acknowledge the hard work the kids have done. Tell them that you're now moving into the data analysis phase.

Step 2 - Review Data Analysis Tools

- Post prepared examples of each tool for the class to see.
- Review the purpose of each tool. Be sure to discuss sample applications.
- As you review each tool, ask the kids if/how the tool might be useful for their project.

Hint: Limit discussion. Intervene if team members begin to discuss the pros and cons in detail. Defer in-depth discussion until you get to Step 3: Tool Selection.

Step 3 - Select Appropriate Tools for Data Display

- Review the data.

    -What does the data tell you?
    -What doesn't the data tell you?
    -Do you have the right data?
    -Do you have enough data?
    -How can this data be used?

- Compare data to each tool.
- Do you want the data to reflect frequency, importance, or impact?
- Do you want to determine the relationship between sets of data?
- Do you want to measure a process over a period of time—possibly revealing a pattern or trend?

> *If a tool doesn't fit, don't force it. Be creative!*
> *Design or customize a tool to meet your needs.*

- Does this data tell you enough?
- Do you need cause and effect analysis?
- Do you need to collect more data?

Step 4 - Graph Data

- Distribute the construction tips for each tool.
- Prepare graphs and charts.

Step 5 - Analyze Data

- Review original project objective and goals.
- Discuss what the data is telling you.
- Do you need more data?
- Determine next steps, recommendations, or conclusions.

Step 6 - Prepare Report

- Pull together and clean-up all important information. Be sure to include:

  -A project statement that includes the objective and goals.
  -A list of team members.
  -A flowchart of your team's process.
  -All products developed during project planning (brainstormed lists, affinity diagrams, or fishbones).

-Sources of data.
-Data analysis charts.
-Recommendations and conclusions.
-Plus/delta on team process.

Step 7 - Present Results

- Have team members share the responsibilities and opportunities to present this project.

  -Present the team's objectives and goals.
  -Introduce team members.

Hint: If it's an entire class project, introduce subgroups within the class—kids who took responsibility for various phases of the project. Remember to include everyone!

  -Provide overview of team process (planning phase, data gathering, team interactions).
  -Present data analysis charts and graphs.
  -Present any recommendations or conclusions.
  -Ask for any questions or comments.

Step 8 - Celebrate!

- Acknowledge the kids' hard work. Provide appropriate rewards and recognition for the team!

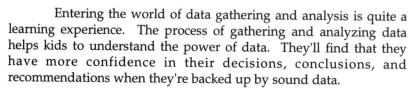

Entering the world of data gathering and analysis is quite a learning experience. The process of gathering and analyzing data helps kids to understand the power of data. They'll find that they have more confidence in their decisions, conclusions, and recommendations when they're backed up by sound data.

But it's even more important to view the entire process they have learned to follow—from planning through data gathering through analysis to final results. The kids are learning an important lesson: paying attention to method or process as well as results is the quality way of getting things done!

DATA ANALYSIS

Data provides kids with the information that they need to analyze a process. These tools will enable kids to investigate the concepts of *variation, common cause/special cause,* and *symptoms* vs. *root causes.* Understanding these concepts will steer kids away from the costly and often time-consuming consequences of *tampering.*

Variation

When studying processes, kids need to understand the concept of variation. Simply put, variation means that a product or process is never the same—it varies or changes continuously. The trick is to determine how much it changes and why!

Root Causes

A root cause is the real source of a problem. Often we deal with symptoms and never understand what is really at the heart of the problem. Fixing symptoms doesn't make problems go away. Sometimes tampering with a symptom makes problems even more complex. *Fixing root causes leads to solving problems!*

Common Cause vs. Special Cause

When trying to improve a situation or a process, it is important to distinguish between special causes and common causes and even more important to deal with them accordingly.

Common cause variation is a situation or event that occurs repeatedly.

Special cause variation occurs sporadically or infrequently and might arise because of specific circumstances.

Tampering

Messing with a process and making changes before you thoroughly understand it.

Think About It

What if a doctor put a cast on an arm without ordering an X-ray? What if the bone wasn't broken after all?

You have to gather data before making decisions!

IMAGINE THIS!

Gathering and analyzing data sound boring. But in actuality, it can be fun and always proves to reveal new insights and interesting perspectives.

Imagine a class of seventh graders—complete with lots of cool, attitude, and humor. For some reason these kids seem to have a hard time completing their work during class. Although the teacher could have quickly rattled off some contributing causes quite accurately, she decided to have the kids do a little investigating.

After asking the kids to share frustrations they experienced when having to complete the work on their own time, she then had them brainstorm a list of causes for poor classroom productivity. Of course the list ranged from boring material and too much work to too much talking and kids coming in late. The list of possible causes was enormous. To simplify matters, the kids prioritized the possible causes to identify probable causes. But this teacher knew that even this prioritized list was not enough. To try to improve the situation by modifiying or eliminating these identified causes without gathering data would be tampering! And, this teacher was beyond tampering!

So, the kids broke into teams to decide how best to gather data for their team's chosen cause. Some teams developed surveys, some created check sheets. After gathering data for several weeks, the kids transferred their information to Pareto, run charts, and scatter diagrams as appropriate. The visual display of data prompted meaningful discussions and some real "ahas" in response to the patterns revealed. As the students identified some improvements they could make and monitor, the teacher, of course, took care of "boring."

WORKING WITH DATA

CHAPTER 5

Working Together

The essential foundation of a high-performance classroom is effective and interactive communication. The tools and techniques that we introduced in the first four chapters are a great start. The ground rules help establish a safe environment, the idea-generating tools provide a non-threatening way for kids to get their ideas out, and the analytical tools bring the thinking process out in the open. Everyone is safe to freely share their thoughts and to openly participate. And, indeed, that's the first step—providing safe vehicles for open communication.

And, the good news is that using these tools and feeling safe to communicate openly starts a learning process that increases a kid's willingness to participate and communicate and, better yet, the desire to do so well. But good communication is not easy. And, although the tools are a great start and provide a safe way to practice, kids need to be taught the interactive skills of good communication.

Listening and talking are as natural as breathing. We all participate with ease. So much so that even as young children we learn to take these activities in stride—take them for granted. And, why not? If we have two ears that hear very well and we've learned to put words together that make sense, what else could you possibly need?

Plenty! And the first step towards helping kids learn to communicate effectively is recognizing that it's not easy—it's not natural. Hearing is a natural sense, but listening is a discipline. It takes effort. But the payoff is tremendous.

Think About It!

Did you know that immediately after the average adult has listened to someone talk, he can only remember half of what he has been told? After forty-eight hours, the recall level drops to 25 percent.

Now, multiply these statistics by the kid factor—radios blaring, peer pressure, friends clowning around nearby. Spooky calculations, huh?

Teachers—more than anyone—recognize the need for good listening skills. In fact, on the standard elementary school report card or progress report, poor listening skills are identified as a common source of poor academic achievement as well as a source of poor social or classroom behavior.

Just so in business and industry. Leaders are finding poor communication to be their Achilles heel—and in particular, the interpersonal, interactive skills of communication. Although we spend more time listening than in any other form of communication, most of us receive little or no formal training. Consider the following information:

Skill	Daily Usage	Formal Education/ Training
Writing	9%	8-12 years
Reading	16%	6-8 years
Speaking	35%	1-2 years
Listening	40%	0-6 months

As you can see, classroom training and education have traditionally focused on reading and writing, considering them to be the primary mediums by which we learn. Very little emphasis has been placed on speaking, and almost no attention is given to the skill of listening. But as the learning process becomes more interactive and the teacher's role becomes more facilitative, the ability to listen effectively becomes increasingly more important and the need to develop these skills becomes readily apparent.

The good news is that kids have the capacity to listen well. And, the learning process can be fun, funny, and a great way to spend time with your class. Some of the activities we introduce to generate an awareness of the listening process and to teach listening skills are as much fun as *Heads up, 7-up; Doggie, Doggie, Where's Your Bone?; and Duck, Duck, Goose!*

The skills and listening concepts that we introduce are fairly basic. Our intent is to create an awareness of listening as a process that kids should approach at a conscious, disciplined level. Although simple, you will find that these skills provide a solid framework from which the kids can continue to increase their effectiveness.

BARRIERS TO GOOD LISTENING

Purpose

A fun and effective way to introduce the concept of effective listening is to start off with the barriers. All kids have certainly been scolded or nagged about their listening. But most kids probably think that listening is something that just happens—or doesn't! Or, even worse, a lot of kids might think that listening is like a personality trait—which means that some kids are naturally good listeners, some aren't.

In order for kids to recognize that listening is a process that is within our control, they need to become aware of not only skills, but pitfalls as well. Once they understand this balance, they can quickly begin to eliminate and prevent the common roadblocks.

On the following pages we introduce activities that will help kids recognize external factors that interrupt the listening process, as well as some listening habits that can indeed get in the way.

Your kids will experience a sense of amusement as they identify their own personal pitfalls—a sense of relief as they quickly begin to see that they are not alone—and, more importantly, an awareness that the listening process can easily run amuck!

Process

Steps for Identifying Barriers to Listening

1. Clue the Class In
2. Brainstorm a List of Barriers
3. Categorize Barriers
4. Breaking Down Barriers

Step 1 - Clue the Class In

- Let the kids know why you are doing this.
- Write the purpose, desired outcomes, and process on a prepared flip chart.
- Post for the class to see.

Step 2 - Brainstorm a List of Barriers

- Write " Barriers to Good Listening" at the top of a flip chart.
- Ask the kids to think about the things that get in their way and make it hard for them to listen.
- Remind the class of the brainstorming rules.
- Kick-off the brainstorming session by sharing one of your own barriers—like too many kids talking at once.

Step 3 - Categorize the Barriers

- Post a prepared chart with the internal/ external barriers and the poor listening habits.
- Review each of the categories.
- Have kids place brainstormed barriers into appropriate categories.

Step 4 - Breaking Down Barriers and Poor Listening Habits

- Have the kids discuss how to remove or control the external barriers. Think about how to deal with some of these barriers in your own classroom.
- Break the kids into groups.
- Assign one poor listening habit to each group.
- Have the group think about when they use the habit, why, and what the consequences are.
- Have each group share their discoveries with the whole class.
- Encourage discussion.

NOTES

BARRIERS TO LISTENING

External

Outside Noise
The sounds of other people talking, cars and machines, music, or even laughter can interfere with our ability to listen.

Physical Environment
Sitting in a hot stuffy room, or a room that's too cold, can keep us from listening—especially if you're sitting in an uncomfortable chair or have no place to sit at all!

Visual Distractions
Looking out a window, at a pretty picture or colorful bulletin board can certainly take our minds away if we're not careful—so imagine what a really radical shirt, an unusual hair-do, or a foxy babe two seats away can do to the listening process.

Speaker Issues
Speech impediments, foreign languages and accents can get in the way of listening. Imagine what an irate or threatening tone could do!

Internal

Personal Concerns
It's hard to listen well if you're worried about a big test coming up, a fight with a friend, or problems at home.

Information Overload
Sometimes our listening shuts down after taking in too much information. It's hard to listen hour after hour to teachers, parents, and friends.

Rapid Thought
Most of us speak at a rate of 25 words per minute, but our brains compute at a much higher speed. We're able to digest up to 600 words per minute. That leaves lots of spare time to think. No wonder energetic kids are tempted to let their minds wander!

Physical Problems
If a kid is tired, cranky, or getting sick—listening is almost impossible. When kids have hearing impairments that prevent them from receiving certain auditory frequencies or hearing sounds at certain volumes, listening will obviously suffer.

POOR LISTENING HABITS
the barriers we create

Pretend Listening- When we pretend to listen, we look the speaker right in the eye, smile and even nod while our thoughts wander right out the window.

Combative Listening - Ready for the attack, we listen combatively and tend to listen only to prepare our persuasive argument or rebuttal.

Defensive Listening - When feeling a little insecure or perhaps even guilty, we hear innocent comments as personal threats or even attacks.

Selective Listening - With so many things to think about and so much to do, it's easy to listen only to the parts that interest us and screen out the rest.

Imaginary Listening - Lots of times we jump ahead and fill in the gaps to make a story whole—whatever the speaker leaves out, we fill in!

Protective Listening - If there's a topic that makes us uncomfortable or embarrassed— like poor grades, an unfinished job, or problems with friends—we tend to tune out, avoid, and forget.

These habits belong to all of us! Count on it! If we're totally honest, each of us could think back to plenty of situations when we've lapsed into these poor listening modes. Depending on our mood or circumstance, it's easy to do and fairly predictable.

We have not introduced these habits to pigeon-hole or label particular individuals. Rather, we have introduced them so that kids can learn to identify situations that tend to trigger poor listening habits.

To really get the most out of these habits, think about them with an open mind, honesty and a sense of humor! The kids will learn a lot as they laugh at the messes we can get ourselves into when we fall into these listening traps!

ACTIVITY

TRY THIS—YOU'LL LIKE IT!

A fun way to quickly engage the kids' energy and get them thinking about the rigors of listening is to conduct this humorous activity. Although this exercise is indeed fun and always evokes laughter, it always proves to be a real eye- opener.

Eye Witness to an Accident

Instructions:

- Ask for five volunteers and have them leave the room. (Make sure they're out of hearing distance!)

- Read "Eye Witness to an Accident" to the rest of the class.

- Explain that you will read this short story to the first volunteer brought back in. Then the first kid will repeat the story to the second kid. The second kid will repeat the story to the third, etc.

- Tell them not to help or prompt the volunteers.

- Invite the first kid to take a seat in the front of the room. (Be sure to tell each volunteer that they can't ask any questions; they just need to sit back and listen.)

- Read the story.

- Invite the second kid to take a seat next to the first. Have the first kid repeat the story as accurately as possible. (Remember, no questions allowed!)

- Record the facts, exactly as told, on a flip chart placed well out of the vision of the volunteers.

- Continue this process until all five volunteers have heard the story.

- Have the fifth person tell his version of the story to the entire class.

- Record. Re-read original story—compare the facts!

ACTIVITY

The Story
For younger kids

You were playing "dodge ball" with four friends during the morning recess at 10:15 on Tuesday. All of a sudden you heard a loud scream and the sound of breaking glass.

Something—either a rock or a football—had gone through the window of the second grade classroom. Two teachers came out of their classrooms to check things out, while the yard duty teacher blew her whistle and came running.

A blonde-headed boy in a red shirt began to cry. Two other boys began to argue. They both were pretty big—and you know that one of them was a sixth grader.

Three girls standing next to the classroom were talking to the principal, one of them was bleeding.

The Story
For older kids

You were standing in the hall talking to three of your friends on Tuesday morning at 10:15—just before third period. Suddenly you heard a loud scream and the sound of breaking glass.

Something—either a bottle or a mirror—had fallen out of a locker just five feet away. Four kids, three of them boys, were huddled together. One of the boys had blonde hair and was wearing a tan shirt and a leather jacket with white letters on the back. Two of the boys were laughing, but one seemed angry.

The history teacher from room 101 came out of his class, while the janitor came running down the hall. The principal was in his office talking to two parents and a secretary.

You heard somebody crying. Someone said that one of the kids was bleeding.

Everyone has fun with this activity—the volunteers up front as well as the kids enjoying the show. The kids will howl as their friends relay the details of the story mixed with the bits and pieces they unconsciously invent to fill in the gaps. When observing this relay chain, kids can quickly see how information gets distorted when the listening process is ineffective.

Begin debriefing this activity by asking each volunteer what approach they used to listen and retain the information. You'll find that each kid has his own process. Also ask the volunteers what made the listening difficult. Remarks like "I was nervous" or "I kept thinking about the kids watching me" can quickly be translated into common listening barriers like stress and mental noise. Involve the kids in the "audience" by asking them to share their observations.

To close this exercise, tell the kids that this was indeed a set-up! This exercise intentionally pits the kids against information overload, disjointed facts, outside distractions and stress. Combining these barriers with the restriction of "no questions" really drives home the importance of interactive listening.

Be sure to thank the kids for a job well done.

LEARNING TO LISTEN

Purpose

Once kids are aware of the barriers to listening, they will begin to recognize that listening isn't necessarily easy and doesn't just happen. Listening isn't easy! In fact, good listening can be hard work.

When learning to listen, kids need to understand that listening is not a passive activity, but rather an interactive process where both the speaker and listener share the responsibility of mutual understanding—aha! effective listening is a team sport that requires training and practice!

With this new understanding, the kids are ready to learn some basic skills. And, although the techniques that we introduce aren't rocket science—they're powerful and will have tremendous impact. Very soon you will be able to see kids practicing and improving their listening skills.

BASIC SKILLS

Focus Your Attention

Concentrating on the spoken word at the incredibly slow rate of 25 words per minute can be difficult for a quick young mind. The key to good listening is to use that spare thinking time wisely. Clearing away distractions, using eye-contact, and mentally reviewing facts or visualizing what is being said help listeners to stay focused.

Clarify For Understanding

Listening is an interactive process. An active listener periodically asks questions to help him understand. This not only helps to pace the speaker, but even helps the speaker make his ideas clear.

Verify For Understanding

As the speaker relays his topic, an active listener should periodically paraphrase the message or repeat key parts in his own words to make sure that he's really understanding the intended message.

Think About It!

Getting rid of poor listening habits is a good start, but replacing them with good listening habits is a must or you'll find yourself slipping right back into the old traps!

Summarize

Both the speaker and listener share the responsibility for mutual understanding. Before walking away, both should work together to summarize key points.

Process

Steps for Effective Listening

1. Clue the Class In
2. Introduce the Basic Skills
3. Facilitate Class Discussion
4. Conduct Skills Practice
5. Get It All Together

Step 1 - Clue the Class In

- Let the kids know why you are doing this.
- Write the purpose, desired outcomes, and process on a prepared flip chart.

Step 2 - Introduce the Basic Skills

- Post flip chart with the basic skills.
- Review the basic skills as a set—emphasize that these skills work together to improve listening.

Step 3 - Facilitate Class Discussion

- Brainstorm the ways that help you focus your attention (sitting still, using eye contact, removing distractions).
- Ask what types of comments or questions they would use to help them clarify what's being said.
- Ask how to verify for understanding. Introduce the skill of paraphrasing and repeating key parts of the message.
- Ask why it's important for the speaker and the listener to review and summarize *together*.

Step 4 - Conduct Skills Practice

- Have kids pair-up in teams of two or three.
- Have each partner think about something he or she would like to talk about.
- Have the first kid share his topic while the other practices the basic listening skills.
- If the team has three members, have the third kid act as an observer and note each attempt to use good listening skills.
- Rotate responsibilities so that each student has a chance to practice.

Step 5 - Get It All Together

- Debrief this activity by asking the kids what they tried to do and how well they thought they did.
- Review all of the basic skills and talk about how they work together to improve listening.
- Remind the kids that these skills are not easy and require practice.

NOTES

Big Words Are Tough!

In our models, key concepts, and skills, we have introduced certain words deliberately because they help to create a mental picture or mental trigger for future use. If the words are too difficult or are new additions to a youngster's vocabulary, translate them at an appropriate level, or better yet, get the kids to help translate! For example, if "combative" is too difficult, ask the kids what they think about when you say "combat." As they respond with words like war or fight, ask them what they think "combative listening" implies.

But, we encourage you to help integrate these communication buzz words into your kids' vocabulary. Building a communication vocabulary will prove to be an invaluable framework for years to come. You know your kids best, so use your own good judgment and be creative.

CONFLICT IN THE CLASSROOM

Purpose

Anytime two people talk there is an opportunity for misunderstanding, confusion, and potential conflict! Conflict is a natural and inevitable part of the communication process. Developing good listening skills, establishing ground rules, posting an issue bin, and using the decision-making tools can and do prevent many conflicts. However, being that none of us live under a rainbow or on Sesame Street, we know that despite all efforts and good intentions, conflicts still come up.

Kids—especially adolescents—have a hard time dealing with conflict. Like many adults, most kids have never consciously developed the skills necessary to handle conflict constructively. More often than not, kids get caught up in the whirlwind of conflict. Some hit conflict head-on. Others tend to ignore issues—trying to avoid awkward or painful feelings.

Helping kids to understand that conflict is a natural part of life that can be dealt with effectively is the first step in breaking down the protective barriers that prevent open communication. As you work with your kids to develop the skills necessary to identify and confront issues effectively, you'll find that the learning process itself gets a lot out on the table and launches you into an incredibly rewarding team-building experience.

Identifying Types of Conflict

The classroom is a complicated creature. And, although to a passing observer, it might look like fun and games, the interaction amongst and between kids is deceivingly complex. Every kid that walks in the door and occupies a desk brings a set of personal concerns, issues, and differences. Multiply that by thirty or so kids and you find yourself in the midst of a powerful current churning with potential conflicts.

As a teacher, you know that it's impossible to channel this current by yourself. The trick is to get kids to recognize and understand what causes conflict so that they can begin to develop the skills necessary to confront and manage conflict on their own.

Learning to identify types of conflict is a skill. By simply having your class generate a brainstormed list, your kids will be learning the first step of conflict prevention—awareness!

Process

Steps for Identifying Conflict

1. Clue the Class In
2. Brainstorm a List of Conflicts
3. Share Key Learnings

Step 1 - Clue the Class In

- Let the kids know why you are doing this.
- Write the purpose, desired outcomes, and process on a prepared flip chart.
- Post for the class to see.

Step 2 - Brainstorm a List of Conflicts

- Write "Conflicts Kids Get Into" at the top of a flip chart. Ask the kids to think about all the kinds of conflicts they encounter in the class, on the playground, or even at home—with other students, teachers, and even their best friends.
- Remind the class of the brainstorming rules.
- Kick-off the brainstorming session by reminding the kids that conflicts happen all the time—everyday. Conflicts range from simple spats to full blown fights.

Step 3 - Share Key Learnings

- Referring to their brainstormed list, have the kids identify which conflicts occur most often.
- Have the kids discuss how these conflicts make them feel.
- Close by reminding kids that conflict is inevitable. Expecting that conflict can be eliminated is unrealistic. Conflict *will* happen in your class, on the playground, and at home.

LEARNING TO DEAL WITH CONFLICT

Purpose

Conflicts— whatever the cause—tend to follow a typical path and progress through fairly predictable stages. Conflicts usually start off fairly mild—with tweaked feelings and mild frustration. We call this the *Yellow Flag Stage*.

Unfortunately, most kids have learned to ignore yellow flags—those early indicators telling them that a conflict is brewing and could escalate. Kids usually choose not to deal with this early stage of conflict because it's not that uncomfortable. In fact, it actually seems more uncomfortable to confront the situation than to try and cope. So kids cross their fingers and hope that things work out or go away.

However, confronting conflict in its early stages can save a lot of headaches, a lot of heartaches—and conflict is so much easier to deal with in the yellow flag stage before tempers have flared and emotions are high.

When yellow flags are ignored, conflict can escalate to the *Red Flag Stage*. "Red flag" conflicts evoke anger, isolation, and rejection. Red flags are tough to ignore, but hard to deal with. To deal with red flag conflicts effectively, kids not only need to employ good listening skills, but also learn specific skills to confront, manage, and resolve the situation. The first step is to learn to understand the escalating nature of conflict and, then, to develop the ability to identify each stage.

COMMON APPROACHES TO CONFLICT

Avoid the Issue   Burying your head in the sand, pretending that conflict doesn't exist, or hoping that it will just go away.

Smooth Over the Issue   Trying to smooth things over or putting a band-aid over the issue.

Win-Lose Attack   Rushing into battle ready to fight. Someone is bound to win, someone has to lose—everyone loses.

Win-Win Resolutions   Working things out together so that everybody wins.

Kids usually have their own style of dealing with conflict. Some kids will rush right in ready to help, some ready to fight. Some kids will try to hide or escape, others will try to negotiate!

Sometimes a kid's style is helpful and appropriate, other times it's not. Kids need to recognize their typical approach to conflict, explore whether or not it's effective, and learn how to adjust their approach to accommodate given situations!

STAGES OF CONFLICT

		Description	Symptoms
Yellow Flag— Early Warning		Simmering Pressure Cooker	Tweaked feelings
		Sparks	Irritation
		Ruffled Feathers	Frustration
Red Flag		Boiling Pressure Cooker	Hurt Feelings
		Fireworks	Anger
		Explosion	Stress
Green Flag— All Systems Go		Smoothed feathers	Mended Feelings
		Open Doors	Shared Understanding
		Smooth Sailing	Confidence

RESOLVING CONFLICT

1. Tell the other person why you are upset.

When telling the other person(s) why you are upset, be sure to stick to the issue, use facts, and avoid jumping *to conclusions.*

2. Ask the other person for their point of view.

Asking for the other person's point of view opens-up communication and lets the other person know that you are aware that there are always two sides to every story. Be sure to use your good listening skills.

3. Review the facts together.

Reviewing the facts together sets the stage for a win-win solution. Make sure you *both understand and check for agreement!*

4. Brainstorm possible solutions together.

Think outside the square—be open-minded and creative!

5. Select a solution that works for both of you.

Sometimes there is a simple solution that you'll both agree on. Other times you might need to work a little harder to find a solution that works for everybody. *Don't walk away until everybody is satisfied.*

Process

Steps for Dealing with Conflict

1. Clue the Class In
2. Introduce Stages of Conflict
3. Conduct Breakout Sessions
4. Share Key Learnings

Step 1 - Clue the Class In

- Let the kids know why you are doing this.
- Write the purpose, desired outcomes, and process on a prepared flip chart.
- Post for the class to see.

Step 2 - Introduce Stages of Conflict

- Post flip chart with stages.
- Review the Stages of Conflict—emphasize the escalating nature of conflict.
- Discuss the symptoms of each stage—check for understanding.

Step 3 - Conduct Breakout Sessions

Break kids into groups of four or five. Have each group :

- Brainstorm a list of yellow flag feelings or symptoms.
- Brainstorm a list of red flag feelings and symptoms.
- Review the steps for resolving conflict.
- Select a conflict to work with.

  Option: Refer to original brainstormed list of conflicts.

- Practice the steps for resolving conflicts.

Step 4 - Share Key Learnings

- Debrief this activity by asking the kids to share what they learned in their group.

REMEMBER THE TOOLS YOU LEARNED

Post an Issue Bin chart in the classroom so that kids have a way to bring up issues in the class. Leave a pad of self-stick notes and markers so that kids who are hesitant to bring up an issue in front of everybody can post an issue anonymously, but resolve it openly with the class.

Try Using a Fishbone to identify the barriers to good communication or common sources of conflict in your class .

- Post four sheets of flip chart paper—two across and two down. Draw a fishbone diagram. Label the bones: People, Methods, Materials, Equipment. You might want to add a tail labeled "Environment." Be sure to title the head of the fish: Barriers to Good Communication or Common Sources of Conflict.

- Leave the fishbone posted in the classroom for several days or even weeks so that kids can continue to add to it. Think about asking kids and teachers from other classrooms to participate!

Use the Affinity Diagram to help kids to identify and categorize conflicts in the classroom. You might want to leave the chart posted for several days before categorizing. This thought-provoking process gets kids to explore conflicts in a safe, non-threatening way.

- Consider typing up the finished product and sharing it with parents or other classrooms.

SUMMARY

Famous Last Words

When first trying to integrate these tools into your classroom, you'll probably find yourself feeling a little awkward. At the very least, you'll find that you need to "squeeze them in" to an already full agenda. Even if you think they're pretty innovative and are anxious to give them a try, they won't seem like a natural part of your process.

Not to worry! That's exactly how we felt when we first tried to integrate them into our own work processes. Lots of the tools seemed well worthwhile and we were more than willing to give them a try. But many a time—especially if faced with a difficult task or demanding deadline—we found ourselves thinking that it might be "nice" to use a certain tool, but we didn't really have the time.

But, one of us—and we won't mention who—always seemed to push and coax until we'd agree to squeeze it in and give it a try. And, you know what we found? This stuff really works! We found our efficiency increased, our energy doubled. We found that these tools weren't just kind of cute and fun, but rather efficient, organized, thorough—tapping into our creativity and knowledge base to produce products and results that even managed to impress us!

It wasn't too long before we figured out that planning them into our work was worth the effort. The time invested up-front was well spent and easily re-captured! We quickly figured out that using these tools actually saved us some time in the big scheme of things—less time spinning, less scrap and re-work, less ambiguity and confusion. And, before too long, the tools weren't something

FROM TEACHER TO FACILITATOR

Malcolm Knowles, a leading authority on adult education, has identified learning principles that successfully engage adult learners in the learning process—incorporating motivations, goals, expectations, and experiences. Knowles found that engaging his students in the learning process changed his role from "transmitter of knowledge" to "facilitator of learning."

As fellow teachers—whether of adults or kids—we thought you would enjoy reading Malcolm Knowles' personal thoughts about the transformation of his own teaching style.

The tools we introduce in this book will naturally initiate interactive learning—engaging your students as you tap into their experiences and incorporate their goals and expectations. Your role will shift from strictly that of the informer to, as Knowles calls it, "facilitator of learning."

We believe that, like Knowles, you too will experience a new dimension of rewards!

I was brought up to think of a teacher as one who is responsible for what students should learn, how, when, and if they have learned. Teachers are supposed to transmit prescribed content, control the way students receive and use it, and then test if they have received it.

That is how all my teachers had performed. It was the only model of teaching I knew… I remember feeling so good when my students did what I told them to do, which was most of the time… I felt psychically rewarded by being such a good transmitter of content and controller of students. I was really a good teacher. ·

My self-concept has changed from teacher to facilitator of learning. I saw my role shifting from content-transmitter to process manager and—only secondarily—content resource.

I experienced myself as adopting a different set of functions that required a different set of skills. Instead of performing the function of content planner and transmitter, which required primarily presentation skills, I was performing the function of process designer and manager which required relationship building, needs assessment, involvement of students in planning, linking students to learning resources and encouraging student initiative.

I have never been tempted since then to revert to the role of the teacher.

Malcolm Knowles. *The Adult Learner, A Neglected Species.*

Schools Are Doing It— And It Works!

Remember that many teachers in the United States are using these tools in their classrooms and experiencing tremendous success.

- Mt. Edgecumbe High School in Alaska is proud of their revolutionary approach and has achieved measurable results.

- A growing number of school districts in Ohio, California, New York, and Texas are integrating these skills, tools and techniques into the classroom. Many are even launching training efforts for their administrators and teachers.

- Colleges and Universities throughout the country are finding valuable applications for these tools and techniques in teaching course content, managing the classroom, and research, not to mention the many uses in administration and services.

that we tried to use or integrate in, but rather—just the way we did things, a natural part of our work!

And, believe it or not, with a little time you too, will find yourself saying, "This stuff really works." But, we fully expect you to have a few doubts and experience a little skepticism as you first read through the various tools and ponder their use in your classroom.

In fact, when we enthusiastically confronted our world of teacher friends—thinking we were offering them the hottest thing since sliced bread—we were hit with comments like, "Gee, this is really great stuff...but it wouldn't work in my class because..." or "Wonderful! You did a great job...but my class is different..." But that didn't phase us. We just shook our heads, smiled, and said, "Try it, you'll like it!"

So, once again, that's exactly what we are encouraging you to do. Hang in there and have faith. In no time at all you will find these tools easy to use and a natural part of your teaching process. You'll find yourself wondering how you ever managed without this new set of skills.

And, after using these tools in your class, not only will you notice a natural, evolutionary change in your own teaching style, you'll also notice a change in your students. Why? Because facilitative leadership breeds facilitative behaviors. As your kids become more and more comfortable with the tools and techniques, they'll begin to take more and more initiative to facilitate effective performance in the classroom. Initiative isn't a personality trait, but rather a matter of know-how. And, these simple yet powerful tools provide just the experience to build that know-how!

As kids become conscious of the listening process, improve their skills and increase their effectiveness, they'll find their confidence bolstered and their performance enhanced. As they work in groups constructing and contributing to a fishbone, flowchart, or affinity, they'll find themselves naturally taking turns and trading off in the leadership role. Why not? It's easy, non-threatening, challenging, and fun.

What you'll find is that you have provided these kids with a set of skills—skills far beyond the basics of reading, writing, and arithmetic. You will have helped these kids to develop sophisticated thought processes and an ability to work together efficiently to solve problems and make decisions. These are the skills that will carry them into the future as capable kids who want to, can, and do!

What's Next?

We're convinced that after trying these tools and integrating them into your classroom you will experience a new dimension of success, a whole new set of rewards.

And, you know what else? We're also convinced that after watching your kids in action and sharing their pride of accomplishment, you will want to expand the boundaries of your own classroom and include others in your experience.

These tools enhance any working relationship and can be used in any situation. We encourage you to use these tools with your principals, support staff, and of course, parents!

Hint: Think about your student teachers or teaching assistants. Wouldn't it start things off on the right track if you worked together to clarify expectations? Can you imagine using the idea generating techniques and analysis tools to plan your lessons—as a team? And, what about working together up-front to establish open, effective communication and learning to resolve issues constructively— what a partnership!

FOR YOUR INFORMATION...

MASLOW'S HIERARCHY OF NEEDS

	Physical Well-being	Safety & Security	Social Affiliation	Self-Esteem	Self-Actualization
Ground Rules		◊	◊	◊	◊
Interviews & Introductions		◊	◊	◊	◊
Expectations		◊	◊	◊	◊
Issue Bin		◊	◊	◊	◊
Plus/Delta		◊	◊	◊	◊

This matrix demonstrates how using these tools to create and manage a participative classroom helps to meet the levels of needs according to Maslow.

According to Maslow, the five levels of needs are physical well-being; safety and security; social affiliation; self-esteem; and self-actualization.

So, as you can see, if you have a warm, dry facility with adequate lighting and ventilation, these tools will help you establish the rest.

BLOOM'S TAXONOMY

	Knowledge	Compre-hension	Application	Analysis	Synthesis	Evaluation
Plus/Delta						◊
Brainstorming	◊	◊				
Affinity Diagram	◊	◊			◊	◊
Evaluation Criteria			◊		◊	◊
Light-Voting						◊
Force Field Analysis	◊	◊	◊	◊	◊	◊
Flowchart	◊	◊	◊	◊	◊	◊
Interrelationship Diagram	◊	◊	◊	◊	◊	◊
Fishbone	◊	◊	◊	◊	◊	◊
Action Planning			◊			

This matrix demonstrates the levels of learning and thinking skills developed when kids use these process tools.

BLOOM'S SIX LEVELS OF COGNITIVE LEARNING

1.	*Knowledge:*	Recall or recognize information.
2.	*Comprehension:*	Organize, rephrase, describe, or illustrate learned information.
3.	*Application:*	Use previously learned material to apply, classify, select, use or solve problems.
4.	*Analysis:*	Identify and think through reasons, causes, motives; determine relationships; analyze and formulate a conclusion using deductive and inductive reasoning.
5.	*Synthesis:*	Combine ideas or related information; produce original communication; make predictions based on diverse data; solve problems, design and plan.
6.	*Evaluation:*	Judge the merits of an idea, process, or solution. Judge, appraise, criticize.

BIBLIOGRAPHY AND SUGGESTED READINGS

Adler, Ronald, B., Lawrence B. Rosenfeld, and Neil Towne. *Interplay the Process of Interpersonal Communication.* New York: Holt, Rinehart and Winston, Inc. 1989.

Bloom, B.S. (Ed). *Taxonomy of Educational Objectives: The Classification of Educational Goals. Handbook 1: Cognitive Domain.* New York: McKay. 1956

Brandt, Anthony. "Teaming with Possibilities." *Parenting.* December/January, 1992.

Brassard, Michael. *The Memory Jogger Plus+.* Methuen, Ma.: Goal/QPC. 1989.

Coate, Edwin, L., *"Implementing Total Quality Management in a University Setting."* Oregon State University. July, 1990.

Cross, K. Patricia, and Thomas A. Angelo. *Classroom Assessment Techniques: A Handbook for Faculty.* Technical Report No. 88-A-004.0. Board of Regents of the University of Michigan. 1988.

Deming, W. Edwards. *Out of the Crisis.* Cambridge, Ma.: MIT Center for Advanced Engineering Study. 1986.

Kagen, Spencer. *Cooperative Learning Resources for Teachers.* Riverside, Ca.: Resources for Teachers. 1989.

Knowles, Malcolm. *The Adult Learner: A Neglected Species.* Houston, Texas: Gulf Publishing Co. 1988.

Scholtes, Peter, R. and Others. *The Team Handbook - How to Improve Quality with Teams.* Madison, Wi.: Joiner Associates, Inc. 1988.

Senge, Peter, M. *The Fifth Discipline.* New York: Bantam Books. 1990.

Tribus, Myron. "Quality Management in Education." *Unpublished Essay.* Hayward, Ca. 1992.

_____ "The Application of Quality Management Principles in Education, at Mt. Edgecumbe High School, Sitka Alaska." *Continuous Improvement Process Information Packet.* Quality Sciences in Education Mt. Edgecumbe High School. Sitka, Alaska. 1990.

For Additional Copies of this Book
Please Complete the Order Form Below,
or Call Our Toll Free Number for More Information

Future Force — Kids That Want To, Can, and Do!
by Elaine McClanahan and Carolyn Wicks

Preparing our youngsters now to become the "thinkers" and "doers" who will lead us into the future is critical. The whole purpose of this book is to educate and train the children of today to deal with and contribute to the ever changing demands of the future.

Translating the tools and techniques of TQM provides teachers with an interactive learning process – a process introducing analytical and technical tools as well as social skills. This interactive learning process helps teachers create a classroom full of kids who want to, can, and do – the Future Force.

(Please Print)   Date _____

Name _____

Address _____

City _____ State _____ Zip _____

Phone (_____) _____

Send order to:
PACT Publishing
3233 Grand Ave., Ste. N-112
Chino Hills, CA 91709
Or call to order:
1-800-858-0579
1-909-792-4143 Fax
1-909-792-0903

PRICE	QTY.	AMOUNT
$19.95		
	Sub-total	
For Delivery in Calif. Add 7.75% Sales Tax		
Shipping & Handling: Min. $3.00		
	TOTAL	

Workshops Available

The authors conduct interactive workshops and in-service days for teachers, principals, curriculum and staff development personnel.

☐ If interested, check here and return this form with your order or call 1-800-858-0579.

For Additional Copies of this Book
Please Complete the Order Form Below,
or Call Our Toll Free Number for More Information

Future Force — Kids That Want To, Can, and Do!

by Elaine McClanahan and Carolyn Wicks

Preparing our youngsters now to become the "thinkers" and "doers" who will lead us into the future is critical. The whole purpose of this book is to educate and train the children of today to deal with and contribute to the ever changing demands of the future.

Translating the tools and techniques of TQM provides teachers with an interactive learning process – a process introducing analytical and technical tools as well as social skills. This interactive learning process helps teachers create a classroom full of kids who want to, can, and do – the Future Force.

(Please Print)   Date _____

Name _____

Address _____

City _____ State _____ Zip _____

Phone (_____) _____

Send order to:
 PACT Publishing
 3233 Grand Ave., Ste. N-112
 Chino Hills, CA 91709
 Or call to order:
 1-800-858-0579
 1-909-792-4143 Fax
 1-909-792-0903

PRICE	QTY.	AMOUNT
$19.95		
	Sub-total	
For Delivery in Calif. Add 7.75% Sales Tax		
Shipping & Handling: Min. $3.00		
	TOTAL	

Workshops Available

The authors conduct interactive workshops and in-service days for teachers, principals, curriculum and staff development personnel.

☐ If interested, check here and return this form with your order
  or call 1-800-858-0579.

For Additional Copies of this Book
Please Complete the Order Form Below,
or Call Our Toll Free Number for More Information

Future Force — Kids That Want To, Can, and Do!

by Elaine McClanahan and Carolyn Wicks

Preparing our youngsters now to become the "thinkers" and "doers" who will lead us into the future is critical. The whole purpose of this book is to educate and train the children of today to deal with and contribute to the ever changing demands of the future.

Translating the tools and techniques of TQM provides teachers with an interactive learning process – a process introducing analytical and technical tools as well as social skills. This interactive learning process helps teachers create a classroom full of kids who want to, can, and do – the Future Force.

(Please Print)   Date _____

Name _____

Address _____

City _____ State _____ Zip _____

Phone (_____) _____

Send order to:
PACT Publishing
3233 Grand Ave., Ste. N-112
Chino Hills, CA 91709
Or call to order:
1-800-858-0579
1-909-792-4143 Fax
1-909-792-0903

PRICE	QTY.	AMOUNT
$19.95		
	Sub-total	
For Delivery in Calif. Add 7.75% Sales Tax		
Shipping & Handling: Min. $3.00		
TOTAL		

Workshops Available

The authors conduct interactive workshops and in-service days for teachers, principals, curriculum and staff development personnel.

☐ If interested, check here and return this form with your order
   or call 1-800-858-0579.